HOMES
& GARDENS

BOOK OF
DESIGN

HOMES
& GARDENS

BOOK OF
DESIGN

MATTHEW LINE

Interior Design Consultant   Simon Cavelle

Editorial Consultant   Karen Howes

First published in the United Kingdom in 2000 by Cassell & Co
Text copyright © 2000 Matthew Line
Design and layout copyright © 2000 Cassell & Co

Homes and Gardens is published every month by IPC Magazines Ltd. For subscription enquiries and orders please call
01444 445555 (fax no. 01444 445599).

Distributed in the United States of America by
Sterling Publishing Co., Inc.
387 Park Avenue South
New York
NY 10016-8810

A CIP catalogue record for this book is available from the
British Library.

Editor Catherine Bradley
Interior Design Consultant Simon Cavelle
Editorial Consultant Karen Howes
Text editor Judy Spours
Indexer Hilary Bird

Design Director David Rowley
Designed by Nigel Soper
Art Editor Tony Chung

ISBN 0 304 35491 0

Typeset in Simoncini Garamond
Printed and bound in Italy by Printer Trento S.r.l.

Cassell & Co, Wellington House, 125 Strand,
London WC2R 0BB

CONTENTS

INTRODUCTION
TO DESIGN

Interior design is about creating a balanced environment in which to live your life

WHATEVER ELSE we may wish them to be, our homes are first and foremost places for living in. We can spend all our spare hours decorating and improving our living spaces, but unless we see them as happy refuges in which to cook, eat, sit, talk, study, sleep and rest they will never be anything more than beautifully decorated, fabulously improved, but ultimately lifeless spaces.

A number of years ago I was sent by a magazine to write about the interior of a large house just outside London. The house had already been photographed and I had seen the pictures. My job was to string them together with text so that the reader could build up a mental picture of how the different rooms jigsawed together and something of why the owner had decorated the house in the way that she had. When I arrived, the house was exactly as the photographer had portrayed it: severely beautiful and untouchable. The style was completely at odds with the enthusiastic woman behind the project who eagerly led me round her black and white rooms – all blindingly perfect, down to the black hairbrushes on the white dressing table and the black buttons in the white Chesterfield sofa. In fact, the picture she had created was such a perfect still life that I could only presume that she lived alone or elsewhere. It wasn't until the end of the tour, when we sat in her black and white kitchen drinking black coffee out of black cups, that she let it drop that she lived in the house with her husband and two young children. A few minutes later, I leant against the wall and fell into a concealed cupboard filled with toys, books, children's pictures, photograph frames and kitchen equipment, none of which was black or white, but all an essential part of everyday living. Twelve beautiful, sterile rooms and one cupboard brimming with life.

There will always be a discrepancy between the way we'd like to live and the way we do. Our homes are both our private space and public face. They are also controllable environments, fun to play with and a clean canvas upon which to project the ideas we have about ourselves. If we want to decorate our home like that of a 19th-century squire, convention no longer prohibits us from doing so. Nor is there anything to stop us from turning a sitting room into a shrine to post-war modernism or a bedroom into a Moroccan souk. And having created our own environment, we enjoy inviting others in to share it, because there is no fun in playing out our attitudes and aspirations on our own. It is only when the dreams overtake the reality, and rooms become stage sets rather than settings for real engagement, that we start to lose a sense of perspective.

While we are in a position to control our environment, we vary in the degree to which our homes balance need with self-image. We recognize that at its most basic level a home is a collection of interconnected rooms, each based around a function, such as eating, sleeping, washing or entertaining. A well-designed home services these functions simply and practically. Yet while we might take an ergonomic view – and place the dishwasher next to crockery cupboards in the kitchen, or choose a hard-wearing carpet for the hall, or put radiators under the windows to heat the cold air as it enters – mood, appearance, habit and convention shape our design as much as functionality. We will hang pictures in a bedroom so that they can be appreciated from the door rather than from the bed – which is, after all, where they would normally be viewed from – because convention tells us that we should do so. And many of us continue to adopt a fireplace as a focal point in a centrally heated sitting room because it is painful to admit that our real focus is now the television.

We also aim to balance our needs and aspirations with the spaces we acquire, but it is rarely straightforward. The 21st century preference for open-plan living with multi-functional space translates easily into new urban loft-style apartments, but the large proportion of us who live in housing built in the 19th and first half of the 20th centuries have only just begun to think about changing the functions of rooms that relate to a long forgotten lifestyle. Without servants, is the best place for a kitchen in the basement? Now that we choose to entertain more casually in large kitchens decorated as smartly as sitting rooms, why keep a formal dining room that we rarely use? And just because historically bathrooms were added to the rear of terraced houses, does that mean that this is the most efficient site for them now?

So to whom do our homes play? Our needs, convention or the expectations of others? Unlike clothes, when we literally wear our aspirations on our sleeve for all to see and change our image on a daily basis according to circumstance, we think hard about the way we express ourselves through our homes. Their design makes a clearer, more personal statement about ourselves and one that needs to be acceptable to the cross-section of people we invite in to share it – all of whom will inevitably have an opinion. As with clothes fashion, it is impossible to sit on the fence. Whatever decorating decision we make will be used to support one person's view and confound another's. We will be categorized as a suitable member of a particular group: as 'arty', 'rich', 'conventional', 'unconventional', 'vulgar', 'typical'; as having a 'good eye for colour' or, God forbid, 'boring'. But none of us really conforms to the identity of one group, so how can we coherently

Conservatories provide some of today's most versatile domestic space. They can be used for entertaining, relaxing, home offices or everyday dining, and offer an engaging affinity with the natural world. Full of natural light yet protected from the elements, they are informal, individual rooms suspended from the daily bustle.

express what is a mass of contradictions? How can we have a personal style, when few of us have a clear picture of ourselves, or clear images of what we aspire to be? We are so heavily influenced by external forces that it is difficult to trust our own eyes and instinct. And if we do trust our own decisions, how many of us have the confidence to carry them through? The decoration of most people's homes is therefore relatively haphazard. It is usually the result of a contradictory collection of new ideas, associations, memories and assumptions. And when self-doubt is added to an equation that involves the choice between an overwhelming number of available colours, fabrics and furniture, it is hardly surprising that so many of us cling to set formulae and plump once more for magnolia walls, a splash of colour on the curtains and sofa, and toss a coin for beige carpet or varnished boards.

If there exists a secret to interior design, it is knowing how to create coherence out of a disparate collection – knowing how to accommodate and cohese a chic new sofa, the drawings your children bring home from school, an antique desk, six-year-old curtains and

Accommodating a multitude of possessions is a challenge to any design scheme. This gallery of pictures includes very diverse shapes and sizes yet remains visually coherent. There is a clear hierarchy in this pattern structured around the large central mirror and echoed in the geometric design of the sofa below.

Auntie Annie's wall hanging that you can't be parted with. An interior design has to make visual sense of the relationship between you, your home, your belongings, your family and, most importantly, the way in which you live your life. This is why the best interior designers look and listen hard, not just to what their clients want but to what they need from day to day. Learning to be objective, therefore, is the first step to designing a living space in which you and your family feel good and relaxed and which has the capacity to raise your spirits.

If the best cookery books show you how to eat, then any book on interior design should show you how to look. Good painters communicate through the sense of sight. This puts them in touch with their subject, their surroundings, themselves and whoever looks at their painting. Likewise, the best interior designers communicate clearly the owner's needs and interests as well as that of the house. Wendy Nicholls, currently Senior Interior Design Director at Colefax & Fowler, once said that in an odd way houses tell you the colour they want to be painted and families dictate the style of surroundings that suit them most. It takes practice to become attuned – to look and really see – but having the confidence to trust your eye is where all design starts.

Because the principles of good design are natural and to a large extent innate, most interior designers would agree that they frequently throw received wisdom to the wind, put down their rule and pen and work from eye and instinct alone. This would seem to imply an irrational approach, but actually the opposite is true. The reason we fly into a panic at the thought of designing a room is because we are overwhelmed by its three-dimensional nature. How can we possibly guess the result when each element, from light to space to colour to quantities, impacts on the others? With so much choice and seemingly no parameters, we don't know where to begin.

Rather than consider the whole, what we tend to do is grab the project from, as it were, a corner. This usually means that we start by plunging headlong into colour charts and fabric swatches, balancing a colour we like with the mood of the room with the vague idea that if it 'matches' it will somehow 'work'. It may well work, but we won't have got the best out of that room at all times of day, because we won't have started by considering the complete picture.

It is good to know that there are parameters in design and that they are not just of our own making, and that there is a starting point to designing a room – and an end. It is also encouraging to know that each ingredient will contribute to the success of the whole, providing that something of the science of this art is understood. Every time we make a colour or fabric choice, we are already working within a scientific framework and making reference to underlying principles of design that we can barely articulate. An understanding of some of these design principles empowers us to do far more than just replicate a style that is, after all, someone else's solution and inevitably bound to

A wonderful rustic bench and table in a beautifully proportioned, classical 17th-century kitchen are complemented by elaborate detailing above the double doors. The look is balanced by a pair of modern Italian ceiling lights over the table. Achieving harmony between old and new is a challenge for interior designers and decorators alike.

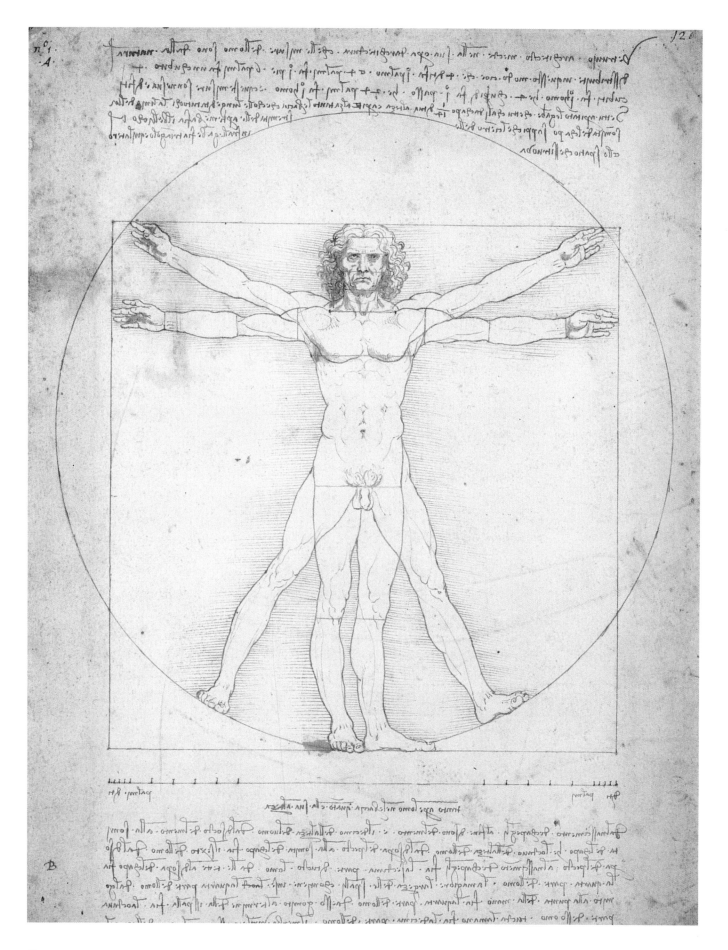

fall short of our own needs. Rather, to create a design that expresses us and our own needs successfully and coherently. We may, for example, be inspired to incorporate a French or Gustavian window treatment in our home. Instead of adopting it wholesale, if we are able to look beyond it and see how it adds height to a window, enhances the width of the architrave or filters light, we are in a position to extract what we need from that design and adapt it to our own home.

When we come to examine the universal properties of space, light, colour and materials, we will be looking at the interplay of the natural laws that govern them. A basic understanding of how some of these laws function in the microcosm of the home will enable us to work with, rather than against, them and help us to predict the end result. It is an holistic approach to design and one based in the fact that we tend to be happier in environments that work in harmony with nature, rather than one that subdues it. Some of the finest Georgian interiors, for example, are highly valued not just for their age and workmanship but also because their proportions mirror those found in nature. The ratio of a room's height to width is based on the principle of the 'Golden Section', a mathematical formula expressed in Ancient Greek, Roman and Egyptian architecture and which was first drawn directly from natural forms (see page 35). It is a formula that occurs in the spiral of an ammonite and in the spiral of seeds in a sunflower that grow smaller as they reach the centre. It can also be found reflected in the proportions of the human body, as famously expressed by Leonardo da Vinci. In the classic Georgian interior the Golden Section has been applied throughout, from the shape and proportions of the chimney breast and windows, right down to the width of a glazing bar and shape of a door handle. The result is that when you walk into those rooms they feel good to be in – all of a piece.

The laws that govern colour (and therefore light) are a constant upon which the designer depends. All colour relationships are based on the natural division of white light as seen in a rainbow. Like each note in the octave, the colours have characters of their own and a relationship with each other. When one is dominant, it has an effect on

Leonardo da Vinci's drawing of 'Vitruvian Man', created *c*.1490, portrays the proportions of the ideal human body. A similar balance of proportions, termed the Golden Section, has influenced architects and designers since Ancient Greek and Roman times. Classically inspired buildings draw upon these scales and dimensions for a visually harmonious effect.

the others. When pure red, with all its attendant qualities of heat, liveliness and joy, predominates – be it in a room or in a flower-bed – its opposite number, pure green, with its soft, melancholic air, becomes its foil. Orange may support red but spar with blue, its opposite number, while mauve and indigo, which share some of blue's qualities, are calm in each other's company. As pure colours are diluted with others so they, in proportion, adopt some of the qualities associated with them.

People naturally enjoy symmetry, harmony and balance, because nature works from a point of equilibrium. While we may enjoy the excitement of an extreme setting, our natural inclination moves us to redress the balance, either by decorating another room in contrast or abandoning the scheme altogether. Sometimes, when a colour scheme is too soft – too mellow, too lethargic – the balance demands to be redressed with a shaft of sharp, contrasting colour – and vice versa. If all fabrics are deep and soft to the touch, we yearn to offset the sensation with crisper, harder textures. The senses of smell and hearing, though more subtle, are not to be ignored either. Their importance is evident when you think of the sounds produced by the brushing together of different materials or of the effect of an echo or clock chime; or the smells of beeswax and potpourri that cloy when they are overused.

The design of a room not only works on the senses, but it also affects the emotions. Whether we are aware of it or not, emotion is our first consideration when we come to decorate. We will say that we want to create a cosy, fresh, intimate or bright room and then pick colours that we feel reflect these moods. While colour plays a large part in evoking

The lucidity and elegance of the Pazzi Chapel, in the precincts of Santa Croce in Florence, derives from a concentration on pure geometric form. Designed by the Italian architect Filippo Brunelleschi from around 1430, this 500 year-old building defines on a human scale the principles of proportion and balance, harmony and simplicity, to which we still respond.

a mood, texture, proportion and use of light can be powerfully combined to the same end. A dark green library with walls blanketed in books, plush red velvet curtains and low controlled light will have a completely different effect on us than the modern white kitchen with a scrubbed table and huge, sunlit French windows. Understanding how each aspect of a design contributes to an overall sensory message that triggers an emotion empowers both architects and designers to manipulate these aspects to great effect.

Some of the most extreme examples of manipulative design features are to be found in cathedrals, in which every detail is designed to evoke awe by playing with our perception of scale. We enter through a small door and thus the building's relative size is magnified. The avenue of arches that marches ahead of us accentuates the building's length, while its shape accentuates its height. Instantly, we are made to feel that we are inhabiting an environment that is beyond our grasp and that demands obeisance. Indeed, all that is most attractive – from carved stone statues to bosses on a vaulted ceiling – is positioned high up. Even the high windows that control the primary light source symbolically only illuminate the upper echelons of the cathedral and throw only the occasional dust-catching shaft downwards into the gloom.

There is a fourth dimension to design, which largely goes unnoticed. We lavish a great deal of care and attention on the creation of an environment. After the painters have moved out and we have heaved our furniture back into a room, there comes a moment when we plump up the cushions and declare it finished, move in and, apart from regularly cleaning it, absorb its assets into our daily routine. While we may accept that its good looks require maintenance and that dents and scuffs will testify to the reality that it is growing old with us, we forget

The elegant neo-classical doorway of Chiswick House in London was modelled on Andrea Palladio's Villa Rotonda by the 3rd Earl of Burlington in 1725–29. The perfect proportions and balance of the building appeal to modern eyes as strongly as they must have done to a contemporary observer.

that the moment in which we start to inhabit the space is the moment it comes alive – by adapting to and reflecting our own characteristics.

Surfaces acquire ornament, furniture shifts to accommodate particular needs, and the room gradually starts to acquire its owner's individual smell. While a room will darken as it reflects neglect, so it will also absorb and reflect back care and attention. We can see this clearly when we walk round historic houses that have remained in the same family for generations. We consciously enjoy the results of fine craftsmanship in the design and detail of the interior design, the furniture and paintings. We also appreciate, but rarely notice, the degree to which its brilliance is kept shining by the attention that has been devoted to it – through both the continuous enjoyment of it and the palpable care in its upkeep. How many of us have admired the deep patina on a wooden table that has been polished daily for centuries, the colour and texture of which no amount of fakery can truly replicate?

We enjoy harmony, proportion, symmetry, balance and care in our surroundings because they are part of our own nature too. They are the qualities that we will often attribute to a 'design classic' and are the reason that we choose to return to such designs again and again, whatever their age. You only need look at the versatility of a simple gingham check or herringbone weave, for example, or at the timelessness of rat-tail cutlery, an anglepoise lamp or a standard wine goblet, to see that these subtle qualities have been realized. Because these attributes are outside time and fashion, good design has an intrinsic longevity as well – it possesses a beauty and integrity that is universally recognized.

Good design is also sustenance. What we create now is destined to feed or starve future generations. Even so, the handing down of a legacy that builds on traditions of good design is not top of today's agenda, because we are currently seduced by attempts to outwit the past. So much in contemporary life is hallmarked instant and disposable. It has led to the squandering of materials, workmanship that is without craft, and design that finds acceptance through commercial criteria alone. And yet we still recognize that contact with good design has the capacity to lift our spirits and enrich the quality of our lives. In spite of its overtone of Victorian paternalism, this belief is the founding principle of many of our art galleries and museums, including that of the largest collection of decorative artefacts in the world, London's Victoria & Albert Museum.

Against the tide of the instant and the disposable there has, in recent years, been a growing appreciation of simple quality in design, no doubt spurred on by a reaction against our excessively decorated interiors of 10 to 15 years ago. Minimalism, while somewhat alien to the comfortable, forgiving English psyche, has invited us to pare back our designs in true William Morris style to those that we find either useful or beautiful. In doing so, this movement has at least given us the opportunity to appreciate shape and form once more, and to value higher quality artefacts in simpler surroundings. An appreciation worth retaining when the pendulum of fashion inevitably swings back the other way.

At first glance, the idea of grappling with abstracts such as beauty, quality, proportion and harmony may not help us to design our sitting room or to choose the colour of the bedroom walls. Nevertheless, it is through an understanding of the laws that govern space, light, colour and materials that we can, in fact, realize these qualities in the decoration of our homes. They will help us to find parameters for our designs and enable us to think more laterally about the possibilities that are open to us. They will also help us to identify the most suitable materials for a particular task from the huge number of products that are now available. Above all, the understanding of these basic laws will go some way towards putting us in control of the design recipe as well as the result.

1

SPACE AND SHAPE

Space is our starting point: the canvas on which we paint our design. Having decided on its function we can use light, colour and materials to manipulate our perception of it and create contrast through line and form. Design techniques help us to maximize the good points and conceal imperfections by changing how we view different features in a room. By understanding the principles of proportion, we can establish an order and hierarchy in a room's decoration and content. Whatever its size or aspect, we can create harmonious space through careful consideration of symmetry and balance.

Left The abstract shapes of sofa and ottoman in this bright, airy room accentuate the unusual window.

UNDERSTANDING
SPACE AND SHAPE

We respond to spaces with our senses and emotions, instinctively aware of the principles behind the design

BELOW An easy chair, positioned informally across two surfaces, provides a visual anchor in this cleverly designed hallway. Such space exists in many homes but is often occupied by built-in cupboards that restrict further use.

CHANGING SPACES

For most of us, our homes are a reminder that we live in an imperfect world. Few apartments or houses are exactly as we would wish – they are too big, too small, too dark, have a terrible view and a door that opens the wrong way. Yet even apparently irrevocable elements of shape and space can be reinterpreted through considered interior design, and every room possesses its own characteristics that can be turned to your advantage.

When you design a room, your starting point will be the space itself and the degree to which it is serviced by light, access and amenities. List its assets and think beyond its present function; changing its use can open up a whole spectrum of new design options. In considering this, remember that no room exists in isolation. Well-designed houses have a flow that ensures a manageable distance to travel between rooms for washing and sleeping, eating and cooking – without positioning key rooms so close together that the principle arteries become clogged. We may balk at the cost and upheaval involved in re-wiring and re-plumbing a bathroom or kitchen, but if the end result makes the living

space more practical, it will have been worth it. We sometimes overlook the fact that it is the fundamental design decisions, not decorative details, that make the real impact.

All areas in a home have potential, and often neglected ones can be transformed by some simple adjustments. The area at the bottom of the flight of stairs shown on the right has become more than a space to pass through. There is a balance of vertical and horizontal lines in the top of the piano and the risers and treads of the stairs. The dramatic angle of the staircase itself introduces a feeling of movement, while the space beneath the stairs seems to have grown to accommodate the piano. The change in flooring divides the relaxed sitting space from the area of movement and purpose, characterized by a harder surface of wood and tiles. These harder materials introduce natural light and lines of perspective to encourage movement and a feeling of depth.

BALANCE AND PROPORTION

Understanding principles such as balance, proportion, symmetry, hierarchy and order will help to establish a set of clear and simple rules. Many are

RIGHT A low wall behind a pale grey wooden bench conceals the stairway of this whitewashed Majorcan farmhouse. Cushion fabrics and latticework panels help to reduce the echo from hard surfaces in a region of flux and activity. The contrast of smooth walls and soft cushions, horizontal and vertical accents, brings both interest and balance to the scene.

The breakfast room at the Sir John Soane Museum in London has been a source of inspiration for many architects since its conception *c.*1810. Soane showed that space need not always be used practically, and his characteristic introduction of top light through lantern and sky-light has a dramatic, elevating effect on the room.

There is a monastic quality to this vaulted room in a German castle which appealed to its owner. The arch highlighted with stripes subtly distinguishes the bedroom from the living area, an effect that is reinforced by the large rug. Placing a Chinese lacquered screen against the far wall, together with carefully selected pieces of furniture, has changed the mood of the room from intimidating to intimate.

introduced instinctively by an owner's sense of what works visually. The value of space for the sake of space, for example, should not be under-estimated, though it is hard to define. The difference between a low ceiling and a high one is in how it makes us feel. It is almost palpable when we move from a low ceiling room into one of, say, double its height – we instantly feel liberated and released into action.

Designers have consistently used space to manipulate emotions, to create a sense of secrecy, to dignify a room or to excite the imagination. The famous pen-dentive dome designed by the architect Sir John Soane (1753–1837) is located in the breakfast room of his house illus-trated opposite. It is a perfect example of how classical geometry can work in a relatively small domestic context. Although the volume of space contained by the dome appears to have no practical purpose, it generates a feeling of uplift for the room's occupants. By allowing the room to escape from under the dome, Soane has given it a lightness like that of a canopy. This conscious delicacy of touch also dabbles with tricks and illusions using glass and mirrors. Per-spective is deceptive; the bookcase on

ABOVE A clever choice of materials and textures can influence our perception of a room. In this bright modern kitchen the stainless-steel work surfaces reflect light and create strong horizontal lines.

LEFT The luxury of a really spacious bathroom tempts many of us to forego a third bedroom and to wallow instead in a vast tub in the centre of the room. A greater sense of space is achieved here by dispensing with curtains altogether and using louvred shutters against the window to control the daylight, balanced by a large mirror to reflect the light still further into the room.

the end wall appears to be the focal point until we notice that the adjacent glazed doors give views into the airy space beyond.

Few of us are lucky enough to have this kind of space to play with, but we can use the principles that it reveals. Think about the area as a whole; if it is longer than it is wide, place furniture to shorten and broaden it, and if necessary create a new focal point. The decorative arch in the room opposite Soane's breakfast room draws attention to the width and, like Soane himself, uses the fabric of the building as part of the scheme. Even though the ceiling heights are dif-

ferent, similar ratios have been used and each space has consequently a similar feeling. The difference is in their decoration; whereas Soane designed with an eye to the furniture from the outset, the vaulted room accommodates different styles of furniture that complement one another and the dimensions of the space.

The impact of a room can be simplified by paring it back to its vertical and horizontal lines. This enables us to understand the order imposed by a particular design, and to recognize the importance of balancing the contrasting elements. If you look at a room through half closed eyes, you will notice the bal-

The locations and sizes of many kitchens are not ideal, especially those in apartments. This kitchen at the top of a 19th-century house in London is limited by the dimensions of the room. The designer has visually exaggerated the length of the wall, keeping the units pale to increase the sense of ceiling height, often low in these properties.

The Jaoul House in Paris, designed by Le Corbusier, illustrates how successfully the choice of materials can influence the design of an entire interior. Bricks, tiles and concrete combine to create an imposing space – highlighted here and there by the strategic addition of a patch of colour.

ance of two effectively opposing forces: the horizontal line is calming, still, horizon-like and distant, whereas the vertical line is dynamic, immediate and challenging. When used together in a considered way, the mixture of the two produces a feeling of harmony.

HIERARCHY AND ORDER

Effective room schemes will favour symmetry and balance, but avoid a sense of uniformity by creating a hierarchy. More often than not, this stems from a leading piece of furniture or feature from which the rest of the design can flow. A hierarchy, however subtle, is essential to the coherence and unity of a design scheme.

The positioning of furniture does not have to follow convention. In fact, an object will often have far more impact if it is prominently sited in an unusual place. As we look past the half-glazed door into the bathroom on page 24, for example, we see a bath that has been positioned centrally to create two separate regions and impose a hierarchy that brings order to the space. Although the kitchen ceiling opposite it is almost as high as that of the bathroom, you can see that because it is considerably wider, the ceiling appears to be relatively low. The unit in the foreground has also been placed to subdivide the space into cooking and dining areas, and the use of reflective materials helps to bring plenty of light into the room (see page 85).

FLEXIBILITY AND FOCUS

When styling any space, it is important to start from a simple platform and build up. Keep your aims and objectives clear and focused. Resist the temptation to go shopping immediately for handles or lampshades, as these details should take their lead from the evolving scheme.

Flexibility, now a major feature in
domestic design as a result of the value
placed on space, should also be built
into any scheme. This may make the
task more complex in the planning
stage, but the design will greatly benefit from being adaptable. Part of good
design is accepting and addressing our
need to use a space in various ways –
often at the same time.

In the clear and uncluttered kitchen
pictured top left, the designer has
thought beyond the aesthetics to answer
practical demands for sufficient storage.
All the paraphernalia normally displayed
in a kitchen has been carefully concealed. In order to break up the long run
of cupboards, a rhythm is achieved in
the repeating panels, echoed by the
repeating jars below. These strong
horizontal blocks balance well against
the floor-to-ceiling window at the end.
Further storage is promised on the top

of the cupboards and the elegant steel
steps provide safe access.

In the interior featured below left, the
architect Le Corbusier has created a
strong lateral movement throughout the
space. A shallow vaulted ceiling is
strengthened by the repeated lines of the
mortar. The rigid, hard-edged, block-
like fireplace counterpoints these
powerful horizontal lines and contrasts
with the curve of the vaulting. This space
works on a more dynamic plane than a
normal domestic space and conse-

quently both elements need to be more
extreme to achieve a balance. The principle that it illustrates, however, can be
used to good effect in many domestic
settings. The effective design of the more
conventional kitchen illustrated above
also features a horizontal bias. The
addition of a fixed steel ladder to access
the wine store at the top of the units
provides a balance between the horizontal and vertical emphasis, as well as
reflecting the rectangular spaces in the
wall units between its rungs.

KEYNOTES

- PROPORTION
- BALANCE
- PERSPECTIVE
- ORDER
- HORIZONTALS AND VERTICALS
- FLEXIBILITY
- COLOUR AND LIGHTING SCHEMES

The drama of a sinuous staircase dominates the domestic cross-roads in this hallway. Only the handrail and soffit are curved – all other lines remain essentially straight, yet the effect is of fluidity and movement. The slight structure enables light to filter down from the floor above to create an impression of airiness and space.

THE ARTERIES OF THE HOME

Every space within a building possesses potential: it has depth and volume; its design is not irrevocably fixed; and as we pass through it we will experience it from changing viewpoints. Therefore the shapes within it will also be viewed from different angles and with different reference points. Most of us have thought long and hard about the design of the major rooms within our homes, while the hallways and landings that connect them tend to be overlooked and rarely considered as interesting spaces in their own right.

In fact, these areas of the home are often the most important 'bridges' and 'crossings' that lead us through the domestic landscape. They are as dynamic and as blessed with an ever-changing perspective as any other space. These areas admit light and air to the home, and passage through them frequently signifies a natural and necessary pause between activities in the enclosed rooms. To see them as dead spaces to fill with built-in cupboards would be a mistake. The quirks of stairwells, skylights and entrance spaces are what give character to the house as a whole and provide insight as to how it was planned and built. Use them as a means of shaping your individual style, but when decorating also consider them as the element that unifies all the other rooms that lead off them. You may choose to work against the design of the other rooms and create a deliberate discord, but do not disregard the connected rooms, as they will always influence the end result.

REACTING TO SPACES

We appreciate a space through all of our senses. When we walk into a room we have never entered before, it is remarkable how quickly we will assess its light, views and smell, as well as its dimensions and proportions in relation to our own stature. We are the reference point for the perception, so as we move around a space the way in which we view it changes.

Most of the information we absorb is visual. We will instinctively assess the delineation of that space and grasp its principle reference points, key horizontal and vertical lines and points of convergence to help us form a perspective. And it is this visual framework which plays a primary role in the way in which we respond to a room.

The other senses are brought into use, too. Texture, which we feel underfoot or by the touch of a hand, will soften lines or give a space depth or height. And the way in which sound bounces off different surfaces can have the most profound effect on our experience of a room. This is particularly noticeable when we come to move house. Just as the carpets have been loaded into the removal van, we discover that a room we thought we knew so well has suddenly acquired a strange echo that is wholly unfamiliar. Smell is a sense directly linked to the emotions, which is why scents such as those of flowers, polish or candles play an indefinable role; like our appreciation of a room's atmosphere – which may relate directly to its past use.

Because we tend to believe our senses, particularly the sense of sight, designers have long enjoyed deceiving them. They do this, for example, by using line and colour to trick us into believing that an area is bigger or smaller, lower or taller, than it really is. This is the reason why those magazine features that show the decoration of one room in three different ways never cease to fascinate us. They clearly demonstrate the extent to which you can manipulate the design of the same space and so manipulate our understanding of its very nature and substance.

ILLUSIONS OF PERSPECTIVE

*Like magicians, we can create visual tricks to
deceive the eye in its perception of interior space*

**A row of mirrored cupboards runs
the length of this studio room in
the barn of a German artist. His**
passion for giving an impression of
austerity obliges him to conceal the
evidence of everyday life in storage
units behind cleverly designed
doors. The reflected space appears
to double the area of the room.

THE EYE OF THE BEHOLDER

If design is about transformation, then
the degree to which designers play magi-
cian is often underestimated. They are
masters of illusion. There are a whole
raft of tricks designers will use – many of
them so subtle they are never noticed,
enabling them to accentuate the positive
aspects of a room or give credence to a
design. To a large extent, they rely on
'perspective', a term that we associate
with fine art. By guiding our eye, its linear structure can be used to challenge
our perception of a space, just as it does
in imagination on a canvas. Such 'illusions of perspective' have been exploited
in interiors with subtlety and skill for
centuries. Designers often use the technique to imply that rooms are bigger
than they actually are, or to delude the
viewer into believing that an architectural feature painted on to a wall is real.
While *trompe l'oeil* views (see page 149)
or still lifes may help to enhance the feeling of volume in a space, as well as
provide an interesting focal point, many
of the devices used are altogether more
subtle means of altering our perception.

In discovering how we view a particular room, it is important to recognize the
degree to which we subconsciously

grasp its linear structure. This is the primary means by which we perceive the
characteristics of a space. Whether it be
the edge of a sofa or a table top, whether
it is near to us and appears large, or further away and appears small, will all be
automatically taken on board and will
alter the way in which we appreciate the
room as a whole. When tackling perspective, remember the basic rule that
many horizontal lines will make a space
feel lower and wider, whilst vertical lines
will emphasize height and reduce the
feeling of width.

The illusion of perspective is particularly influential when we see lines that
run parallel to our line of vision or that
stretch away from us. These lines appear
to converge as they become more distant. The more of these lines we
introduce into a room, the longer the
room will feel. For example, the next
time you are in a room with a stripped
floor, notice which way the floorboards
run and see how the lines that they produce serve to emphasize the area's length
or depth. The more we appreciate the
effects of perspective, the more we can
use it to strike a balance within a space,
exploiting its best features and playing
down its weaknesses.

The use of mirrors can dramatically change the way in which we perceive a room. Clearly, great care must be taken in introducing an element that will visually double a space and considerably increase the volume of light that is bounced around. A large slab of glass can be difficult to live with, expensive and may overwhelm the room's other features. One solution is to use the mirror in panels so that diagonal lines are introduced into the space. Such a strategy, adopted in the space illustrated on the left, has brought more light and a feeling of lateral space into this long room through what at first appears to be a screen. The diamond pattern is used effectively here, as it does not seek to promote height or extend the already long room. Instead, it sets up a rhythm down the length of the space and gives the large room definition and context.

Windows are a natural focal point in any room, and their treatment will influence how we perceive the space. The height of these elegant windows is enhanced by the long curtains, sheer enough to allow plenty of light through. Repetition of the small panes in a vertical arrangement also strengthens our awareness of height.

USING LENGTH AND BREADTH

Most techniques of illusion work to maximize the natural attractions of a room. The greatest asset of the room illustrated on the previous page is clearly its windows. Their impact has been enhanced by hanging simple but powerful full-length sheer curtains that both accentuate the height and allow as much light as possible to pass through. These four sets of curtains work like classical columns and focus attention upon the bright, airy view beyond, as well as emphasizing the grand proportions of the simply decorated room. The vertical up-thrust used so successfully by Gothic architects is employed to great effect here, creating a sense of openness and release. The choice of polished floorboards has made the most of the natural light that floods into the room.

Illusions of breadth and depth can be as important as those of height. The well-balanced kitchen pictured above uses techniques of perspective to expand the length of the room. At the far end, the open, curtainless French windows play down the division between inside and out, and the arrangement of furniture beyond continues the feeling of progression. The table outside provides a focal point for the setting. This is an architectural trick of creating an axis, an imaginary line which encourages not only a vista at each end, but also movement between two points – the table and the point at which we are standing. The sensation of space is encouraged by the soft, contrasting background of the garden beyond, which suggests that the area extends perhaps further than it does.

A common problem that occurs is the unwitting use of this technique of perspective. This may be detrimental to a particular space. Many older houses, for example, have had their two main ground-floor rooms opened into one; two regular spaces have thus become one elongated room. While this is not in itself bad, its decoration needs to be considered carefully so that the long and narrow space is not accentuated. In buildings of the 19th century, the dado (or chair rail) and picture rail are often reinstated for authenticity and subsequently treated, as were the originals, in contrasting colours. These different horizontal lines on the adjacent walls produce strong lines of perspective. They create the illusion that the space is even longer and more awkwardly narrow than it actually is.

THE GOLDEN SECTION

Ancient Greek philosophers and mathematicians – and their counterparts in Ancient Egypt – were fascinated by the geometry of the natural world. Repeating and symmetrical patterns, such as those on a butterfly's wing, as well as harmonious proportions characterize design in nature. One of the Ancient Greek theories that has stood the test of time is that of the 'Golden Section' (also termed the Golden Ratio, the Golden Mean or the Divine Proportion). This is a means of dividing a certain length in such a way that the ratio of the longer part to the original whole is the same as the ratio of the shorter part to the longer divided part. Considered to be one of the 'two treasures of geometry', this equation has intrigued mathematicians and artists over centuries.

The Golden Section was a key principle of Greek architecture, relating the measures and proportions of structures and columns to those of the ideal human body. Regular ratios govern the relationship of column height and diameter, reflecting those between a human head and body height.

Present in both music and architecture, the Golden Section features in many designs. It appears in the ancient Parthenon in Athens (constructed on a ratio of 4:9) and in Stradivari's violins, as well as the work of many famous artists and composers. Leonardo da Vinci expressed the proportions most famously in his drawing of 'Vitruvian Man' (see page 12), which sections out the human body in ideal proportions. The Golden Section became a vital element of classical architecture and influenced many of the architectural styles that followed. Often claimed to be aesthetically superior to all other proportions, it enjoys a lasting importance in art, architecture and design – indeed, in all harmonious manmade forms that seek to please the eye.

Minimally furnished and reflecting the owner's predilection for a Japanese lifestyle, this central London loft apartment has successfully created a series of living areas in what is effectively a very small space. The retracting Japanese screens and free-standing shelving visually divide the room into living/eating and sleeping areas, the whole unified by a concrete floor painted a dark blue.

KEYNOTES

- LIGHTING TECHNIQUES
- PROPORTION
- VERTICALS AND HORIZONTALS
- PATTERN AND SCALE
- RHYTHM AND REPETITION
- FLOORS AND WALLS
- ADVANCING, RECEDING COLOUR

Interestingly, you do not need large spaces to employ striking visual concepts. Sometimes their impact is greater over a relatively localized space, particularly one which is regularly moved through and viewed from different angles. The 'D-ended' stairwell of Hill House in Glasgow, illustrated on page 33, is an instance in which the designer Charles Rennie Mackintosh has cleverly manipulated space by using the illusion of perspective. We view the space along the handrail, which becomes the screen wall. The strong linear intervention of this wall accentuates the length of the room. It is also interesting to note that the dark wall panelling sets up a false horizon, complemented by the lighter wall above. The Mackintosh design carpet, with its geometric patterning, adds an important accent to the illusion of perspective in the space.

SETTING UP A DESIGN RHYTHM

If we are designing for a large area, we frequently need to control the impact of perspective but simultaneously maintain the free and open feel that it produces. Often the building itself will give us clues as to how we can reduce the sense of being dominated by the space. One trick is to introduce a repeated element that sets up a rhythm, restrains the eye and gives the room a calmer, ordered feel. This also serves to bring a large room down to a more comfortable and inhabitable domestic scale. In the contemporary apartment illustrated opposite, for example, we can see how the rhythm created by the architecture of the building has been used to position the furniture and screens. The piers that carry joists across the ceiling clearly set a natural sequence to the space, and this recurring framework has been used very

LEFT **Large sofas can feature as low level screens to establish different regions in a room. White fabric** covers ensure that the demarcation does not disrupt the attractive light and airiness within the overall area.

RIGHT **Often the most adaptable room in the house, a bathroom's shape can reflect individual taste.** This roll-top bath has been placed directly beneath the skylights in the roof, and a shower behind a waist-high wall tiled in sealed sandstone.

FLOORING IN PERSPECTIVE

Perspective in a room is not only the province of windows and walls, however. The way in which flooring is laid can make a great deal of difference to a room's perceived depth. Try to think of the different effects that can be achieved by changing the bias or angle of a simple flooring pattern. For example, the use of diagonals in the pattern can shift the focal point and expand the apparent width or depth of the space. This is a good technique to employ in narrow areas like hallways. Floor features such as rugs may also be used to complement existing lines, as illustrated in the bathroom opposite, reinforcing the visual coherence of the space.

Floor tiles are a common means of extending or reducing a room's size. Consider first the view from the entrance and the ways in which the lines affect the perceived dimensions of a room. Then think about the relative proportion of an individual tile to the overall space. The bigger the tile, the smaller the space will seem – but the greater will be the pattern's impact. With very small tiles, the impact is so reduced that they become almost insignificant and the pattern will appear closer to a texture (see page 210).

Flooring has become more adventurous, particularly in small rooms such as bathrooms. Chequered tiles make a bold pattern that introduces a sense of movement and drama into the space.

effectively as the basis for the furniture arrangement. Although it may seem logical, this method of balancing architecture with the disposition of furniture is often overlooked. The position of each piece is a coherent reaction to the shell of the building.

Large spaces with a strong illusion of perspective may need to be made to feel more comfortable and less severe without physically closing down the space. The large room pictured above has been subdivided into two regions: a conversation area and an arrival area. The feeling of openness is maintained and the bright window catching the eye heightens the feeling of perspective. It is interesting to see that the elevated planter, which dominates the window, continues the perspective theme and seems to act as the focal point of the view.

SPACES
WITHIN SPACES

Areas within a large space need to have balance and equilibrium, but to retain individuality

RIGHT The alcoves and vertical niches in this long, rectangular room bring a sense of drama and mystery to an otherwise contained shape. Used for storage or decorative effect, they provide contrasting forms and a stabilizing rhythm.

DIVIDE AND RULE

There is no denying that it is much easier to design a room that has one function than a larger space that needs to incorporate a number of individual areas. These may be purely decorative – a slightly more formal area in a sitting room, for example – or designed for a different purpose altogether. A living room may have an area set aside to form a home office, or a calmer dining area may need to be carved out of a busy kitchen. When this type of spatial rela-

tionship exists, it is important that the decorative scheme takes into account the influence of one region upon the other.

Different functions will often dictate a change of pace and dividing lines may be implied in various ways, from the discreet to the dramatic – pieces of furniture, different decoration and colour, lighting effects (see page 90), screening or changes in floor levels. Texture is an important boundary marker: a large rug, for example, is often used to define a conversation area within a larger open

space. The impact of each area on another has to be thought through both practically and aesthetically. The close proximity of a study area to one of high activity or noise could be disruptive, and partition walls or more substantial screening may be the only solution.

In the living room pictured below left, a sofa has been placed to create an area in which conversations can comfortably take place. Its position, set across the room with its back to the entrance area, clearly delineates one space from the other. A console table has been placed in front of the sofa to anchor the piece visually while providing a screen. The table also sets up a focal point that is strengthened by the two chairs positioned on each side; this also invites the viewer to see the nearer space as a more formal seating or dining area. Two separate areas have been clearly created just by

LEFT Multiple use of space is an important element in many modern rooms. Furniture shapes the impact of this relatively ordinary living room, dividing the area by function. In the process, the sculptural qualities of the chairs become more important than their stature.

LEFT A Gothic cupboard above a radiator in a bathroom is used to store bath oils and nightclothes. Following the line of the radiator below, it is decorative as well as functional in a small space.

RIGHT A mezzanine has been incorporated into the Gothic arch of this soaring living room in a former 19th-century school. Its dramatic emphasis is complemented by sleek white walls and richly textured furniture. The rooms are unified by Russian oak flooring throughout.

the way in which the furniture has been arranged. This maintains flexibility and allows both areas to benefit from the open and light feeling of a larger space.

Very large spaces such as lofts are favoured for their airy, liberating feel, but invariably prove difficult to make cosy and intimate. Only by grouping furniture into conversation areas can you hope to translate the daunting openness of the space into a more comfortable social scale. Public arenas, such as restaurants, cafes, even airport lounges, are a good illustration of how a large and potentially unmanageable space can be broken down into several smaller, more accessible areas.

The dramatic setting of the open room on the previous page illustrates the same technique in a strongly architectural context. The hard edges of the furniture also create their own areas of space, echoing the floor to ceiling openings and small niches along each side, and the stark geometry of chair and table legs and surfaces. The dominance of hard lines and suspended rectilinear boxes is offset by the softer curve of the

curtain fabric, providing a strong focal point of light to the room.

On a smaller scale, niches and alcoves that often exist as a consequence of an architectural feature can be used in a number of ways to benefit a space. They can set off a picture or a piece of furniture or be employed for low- or high-level storage. Yet while alcoves that flank a chimney breast look almost heaven sent for bookcases, by building into such spaces you run the risk of losing a room's individuality.

THE IMPACT OF COLOUR AND LIGHT

When you are working on spaces within spaces, it is important to recognize that their decorative treatment will reduce or increase their influence on the room as a whole. The use of a strong colour will draw attention to them and they will begin to dominate the larger area; a paler colour will tend to make them feel that they are receding from the main room, thus increasing the sense of space. Lighting can bring an extra flexibility to these areas and a whole new dynamism to their influence on a room. Mirrors can

also be used to great effect to imply that the room continues or has greater depth than it really has.

You can link these smaller areas both visually and spatially with the larger room, but the smaller, contained spaces will normally rely on the larger one to extend their relationship to the other rooms in the house. A hierarchy will develop between each of the spaces that exist together; this can be shifted or adjusted by the way each is treated – perhaps simply by lighting one area and dimming the lights in another. Although it is important to be brave when taking an idea forward, consider when the room is to be most used. If it is the main living area, take care with the extent of decoration, as the space will need to be able to work throughout the day and in different light levels.

When considering the role of spaces within spaces, the aim is to achieve a balance. If this balance is too perfect, the space will feel contrived and lacking in interest; we are, after all, attracted as much by contrast and sparkle as by calmness and harmony.

RIGHT **In the bedroom at Hill House outside Glasgow, designer Charles Rennie Mackintosh punctuates the** white decoration with a repetitive stencilled theme on shutters, bedhead and bedroom furniture, unifying the different areas of a large and unusually shaped room.

If the space contains an element of discord in its structure, then in order to balance and make it palatable – or even enjoyable – the other elements need to be played down. In the room illustrated on the preceding page, a bold note of discord has been struck in a separate new space added to the original, almost church-like room. The new floor intervenes at a crucial point of the original architecture and exists almost in spite of its surroundings. The decoration is deliberately understated and does its best to play down the violation of the structure. The palette is monochromatic and the wood and leather finishes try to draw your eye away from the uniformly painted walls. Glowing candles tempt us to look beyond the overhanging upper floor and encourage a sense of harmony.

Textures can also play an important role in shaping a more fluid, yet distinctly defined, area. An easy and flexible way of creating a space within a space is illustrated on the left with a simple bed hanging. The fabric, which is draped over a suspended rod, offers the bed privacy and injects a cosy, intimate feeling to the space. This clean, unfussy technique could easily be adapted to a contemporary scheme.

The introduction of a different shape of space need not disrupt a room's overall harmony, but it will tend to promote the differently shaped or sized space above the others. An illustration of exactly this occurs in Hill House in Glasgow, designed by Charles Rennie Mackintosh. The barrel-vaulted space pictured above creates an interest and

gives importance to the bed area over the other spaces. The cool, calm colours that are used here counterpoint the excitement and interest stimulated by the shape and form of the space and furniture. If a strong colour scheme was used, the balance would be disrupted.

The important consideration in dealing with smaller defined areas is of how the room looks overall. If one space looks fantastic but the adjoining area is displaced or suffers as a consequence, the overall scheme is not a real success. This thought should be held and applied to the whole of a house or apartment, since no one room exists as an island, separated from its neighbours. If we do not build their mutual influence into our planning, the overall impact will be disjointed and will inevitably fragment.

COMPLEMENTING
CURVES AND
HARD EDGES

*Flowing and geometric shapes can work together
to create a visually balanced space*

**Here is an example of how a strong
architectural feature in a room
can be balanced by the clever** choice of colour and soft furnishings. The cream sheers at the
window cast diffused light evenly
over chair and ottoman, softening
the hard lines and shadows of buttresses and table edge.

THE ATTRACTION OF OPPOSITES

Trying to achieve a balance between horizontal and vertical lines is a challenge
similar to creating a balance of colours
within a decorative scheme. The relationship between a curved and a straight
line can be a complex one: some curves
complement one another and others do
not, depending on their size and position. In the room on the right, strong
and dynamic angles are softened by the
gentle curves of the easy chair and foot-
stool. The angles of the architecture are
echoed in the defined block of the table,
but these are in turn restrained by the
larger and softer furniture. The powerful
structure of the room is then treated in a
gentle matt white, while its furniture is
brought up in the stronger colour.

Like complementary colours (see
page 117), the juxtaposition of curved
and straight lines creates both balance
and dynamism in a space. These can
work on a relatively small scale, as shown
in the arrangement illustrated top right.
The strong linear edges of the picture
frame are echoed in the horizontal thrust
of the ornamental bowl. Both reflect the
plane of the console tables, even as their
curved edges bring intriguing individuality and movement to the scene.

A table sculpture entitled 'You and Me' and designed by Garouste & Bonetti has a single ceramic pod as its only adornment. It allows the harmonious shapes of sculpture and table to be seen and appreciated in serene isolation.

On a larger scale, the remarkable space pictured on the following pages illustrates the interaction of curves and straight lines more clearly than we might see in an ordinary room. The giant twisting bulkhead introduces a powerful sensation of movement and is both restrained and promoted by the strong repeated joists. These in turn reflect the linear flooring, which itself increases the feeling of perspective. Both of these straight and curved lines run in opposite directions to each other and establish a dramatic but balanced space. It is interesting to note that the key colours used – orange and purple – are complementary, but are prevented from becoming overpowering by the pale floor colour. Further elaborate, softening curves are introduced with furniture and accessories to pick up and repeat the concept.

Although most homes do not have the luxury of such space, we can nonetheless create harmony and interest by introducing curved shapes into a predominantly square scheme. Accessories and details are a good way of bringing in contrasting shapes, perhaps in unexpected contexts, such as bathroom or kitchen fittings. Textural contrasts are also worth bearing in mind to break up a geometric space.

THE IMPACT OF ART NOUVEAU

The exponents of the Art Nouveau movement in the late 19th and early 20th centuries were masters of organic shapes and curves in what is, after all, a predominantly square and boxy environment. They were fascinated by the potential of materials and shapes, endeavouring to find a natural fluidity and movement in whatever they did. A common, and very contemporary, reference point for this style is its link to the forms and shapes found in nature. In continental Europe, designers transformed whole interiors, including fabrics and tableware, into a composition of organic lines, drawing upon twists, curves and tendrils. The balanced tension between curving and straight lines may be very effective in details and motifs – handles to cupboard doors, ornamental features or light switches can be a way of bringing in a curve or softer line into a scheme. Such elements will gain in strength through repetition, and should be used throughout the home.

Their sense of movement makes curved motifs particularly effective in parts of a house that accommodate activity and transition, such as halls and stairs. In the harmonious room illustrated on page 48, the combination of a straight-legged table and curved *chaise longue* is both simple and elegant. To confuse our appreciation of these lines with any further adornment would have destroyed the graceful effect. A calm, contrasting backdrop allows us to enjoy the shapes clearly, offering uninterrupted sight of how the curved back of the *chaise longue* repeats the curve made by the staircase. The flowing, interwoven pattern on the rug's decorative border helps to anchor the two pieces without being too dominant.

Curved accessories, and particularly large pieces of furniture like cupboards, can have a powerful effect upon a space through the juxtaposition of soft with straight lines. Such pieces tend to be expensive, however, as they frequently need to be made to measure – the best way of achieving a harmonious result. The effect of the soft line against a hard-edged working surface will change our awareness of this often neglected area of space. Materials are also an important consideration (see page 154) and in deciding on those you should consider whether you want the area to be dominant or discreet. Keep in mind, too, how

The luxury of a vast living area allows us to display the shape of furniture to best advantage. In this dramatic space, the curves and soft edges of the seating arrangement are isolated on a graphic rug in the centre of the room. The huge curving bulkhead continues to dominate the dining space.

KEYNOTES

- HORIZONTAL AND VERTICAL LINES

- CONTRASTS OF SHAPE AND FORM

- COMPLEMENTARY COLOURS

- VARIATIONS OF TEXTURE

- REFLECTING, ABSORBING LIGHT

- REPEATING PATTERN MOTIFS

- USING ARCHITECTURAL FEATURES

ABOVE **This contemporary staircase emulates the soft curves redolent of the Art Nouveau movement. Its** shapely, sinuous banister brings visual interest and focus to an otherwise rather static hallway.

LEFT **The soft, feminine form of this Art Nouveau sofa echoes the line of the stairs ascending above it. The** pattern for the edge of the handmade carpet was in turn inspired by the ornate banister.

it will work with other fittings and fixtures, and remember that the space will have to work practically. This is especially important in a small area where many tasks have to be undertaken in close proximity. A round kitchen sink, for example, can look fabulous against the hard edge of a counter top, but if you cannot fit your roasting dish in it, the design is flawed. Do not despair in such a case as aesthetics have a way of winning through; you will often find a more practical sink that still has an element you can use to balance the look.

RIGHT **A gently bow-fronted wall cabinet provides maximum storage space in a small corner fixture.** Quite a surprising amount of extra shelf space is acquired with a rounded, rather than a flat-fronted, design.

SMALL AND
DIFFICULT SPACES

Even apparently awkward rooms have character and can be made to work to your advantage

Attic conversions can provide additional bedroom space, and the inherent quirkiness of building into the roof gives these rooms their character. Placing the bed in a position where you are least likely to hit your head is obviously a priority, while other furniture should be low to fit into awkward corners. Since wardrobes and tall cupboards are unlikely to be practical, alternative clothes storage could be old leather or lacquer trunks, doubling up as bedside tables.

DEFINING THE PROBLEMS

Most homes contain some spaces that are difficult to use well, perhaps because they are small, of an awkward shape, or have inadequate natural light. To pinpoint an often instinctive sense that a room is not 'working', it is important that these areas be addressed first with a detailed look at their dimensions.

For example, a space may be simply too small for its proposed use. Although there are many ways to organize and arrange a room, we need at some point to acknowledge its physical constraints. Flexibility is important as it may be necessary to rethink the space allocations through the house or reduce the demands made on a particular area.

The bedroom featured above has been built into the eaves of the roof space of the building. Although the space is quite generous in size, it is awkward because of the roof line. The horizontal emphasis in the line of the bed, table and square chairs is balanced by the verticals of the legs and glazing bars. This reinforces the feeling of the rectilinear space and attempts to redress the angled roof line. The ceiling is treated with a white matt paint to make it 'disappear' as far as possible, but the angles are reinforced visually by stopping the plaster short of the roof structure. This picks up the line of the roof and makes a feature of it in a light, airy way, rather than totally denying the problem exists. The

49

LEFT Some kitchen areas are just the wrong shape to indulge in the sleek look of fitted units, but they can be just as successful by simply placing the elements individually around the room. The relationship between cooker, fridge and storage shelves is maintained by a uniform colour or material.

RIGHT Kitchens should be designed to take account of our individual culinary habits, with the sink and oven reasonably close together and work surfaces within easy reach. The size of this kitchen allows room for a central unit providing additional storage and surfaces for food preparation, which has been designed in the shape of a sailboard.

natural light entering the room has been used to maximize the feeling of space, and the choice of pale reflective flooring and rugs bounces the light back into the room. Low furniture has been used where the ceiling is low, but attention is drawn to the full height of the bedroom by the introduction of an elegant chandelier. The calmness of the colour scheme counterpoints the dynamic geometry and achieves a sense of harmony within this awkward shape. The trick to designing difficult spaces like this is to redress the balance by calming the dominant features of the room rather than fighting against them.

THROWING LIGHT ON THE PROBLEM

When assessing your space, try not to look at all the things that you don't like about it, but focus instead upon what it is you wish to emphasize. One of the most precious things in a room is natural light. When thinking about the finish that you want, and the materials you prefer, do not overlook the way in which light works in the space. This is just as important in a functional area as a relaxing one. In the kitchen area above, space is clearly limited, but stainless steel has been used to clad the wall behind the cooker. The choice is not only practical, but reflects the light coming in from the

window, thus increasing the impact of light within the room.

Although the kitchen on the right opens onto a larger area, we can extract from it some ideas about working with long narrow spaces. The kitchen possesses a large window, which feeds the space with natural light. Positioned on the long wall rather than one of the short walls at either end, the window reduces the perspective that would otherwise make the room feel longer still. All the tall units are concentrated at one end, which brings the end wall visually closer, simultaneously reducing the feeling of constraint. The oven and hob arrange-

KEYNOTES

- INTRODUCING HORIZONS

- STRENGTHENING FOCAL POINTS

- MAXIMIZING DAYLIGHT

- POSITIONING OF MIRRORS

- CONSIDERING COLOUR

- IMAGINATIVE STORAGE

- NEW WALLPAPER

BELOW This sleeping area is a conveniently placed mattress on a platform above the dining area of a small loft conversion, a cube of space created in the void of the ceiling. The long window extends up from below, giving the bed area plenty of light and the useful inset storage boxes echo the shape of the platform itself.

LEFT Occasional bedrooms can be created in areas that would otherwise serve no useful purpose. If not intended for continuous use, these sleeping areas can be platforms or mezzanines accessed by narrow ladders, eyries under the roof where there is just room for a daybed and side table.

ment is offset from the axis that has been set up by the units (see page 32), again preventing any lines of perspective from continuing too far and thus seeming to shorten the room. The floorboards are set across our line of sight and effectively broaden the space between the units, as well as creating a rhythm that reduces the feeling of distance. We still have a long kitchen, but it feels a balanced and harmonious space, rather than disproportionately long and narrow. As with all rooms, kitchens need to be efficient and safe as well as aesthetically successful. On occasions these two aims will clash, but resist the temptation to sacrifice safety for good looks.

Long slim rooms are a common problem, often a consequence of two rooms being knocked together to form one long narrow space. Sometimes the new dimensions of such rooms make them impossible to work as one single area. We therefore need to consider the room as two 'adjacent spaces', planning what functions would suit each part. Do not, however, be tempted to force the rooms together if they really do not work.

SPACE AS A FEATURE

Space does not have to be used to practical benefit. In fact, retaining a volume of apparently 'unused' space can bring extra interest to a room. The upper floor illustrated on the left has been built into the eaves of a building, with natural light borrowed from the windows below giving an optimistic and attractive uplight to the room. It is tempting to build storage into an awkward shaped space, but here this has been resisted to highlight the room's unusual structure.

A large, generous space needs to be treated with furniture of a suitable scale; small pieces will appear overwhelmed. A small room, by contrast, will usually appear more spacious with smaller furniture, unless you use the technique of oversizing. By placing a single item, such as a bench or settle, in a hallway or building a window seat on a landing you can make an enormous difference to how the space is perceived. No one may ever sit on them, but the idea that the area could be used to rest will give a calmer feeling to the space and slow the feeling of movement down. The bedroom area above is simply arranged and the large lateral space is broken down with the repeated grid of the bookshelves. This is potentially a difficult room, again existing as a raised area within a larger space, contained by

screening walls. Warmth and human scale is brought into the room by the books, which anchor the almost floating sleeping region. The strong horizontal beam lines and wall tops emphasize the width of this large, light space.

All surfaces, both vertical and horizontal, should be treated thoughtfully. For example, a huge wall will look best with a larger scale picture, rug or hanging on it. A number of pictures grouped together in a defined hierarchy will have the same effect. React to what you sense the space is demanding. Sometimes, in a small apartment, an oversized piece or painting can introduce the feeling that it is part of a much larger space. Although apparently contrary to standard principles, a sufficiently powerful oversized item will dominate the room. Visually, it creates the illusion that space follows

and works around the object, rather than the other way around.

A small kitchen-breakfast area illustrated above is given the feeling of space by maximizing the amount of natural light in the room. As a mezzanine, the room draws light from above and below the stairway and from the large windows at the far end of the room. An imaginative choice of materials also increases the light in the space – reflective brushed steel for the cabinets and glass for the table top and the screen wall. Although the area has been 'carved out' from the main flow of movement on the stairs, it is cleverly anchored by the solid wooden furniture and complementary right angles of table and chair legs, glass blocks and two ladders. The room thus provides a place of stability and relaxation rather than transience and speed.

Kitchen/diners are a practical combination, especially if space is limited. The glass-topped bar area in this kitchen is a effective division of space, allowing room to sit and relax in a busy overall setting.

STRATEGIES FOR STORAGE

*Contemporary storage is decorative as well as
functional, designed as part of the whole scheme*

Kitchen design continues to strive
for perfection and the storage
ideas, detailing and materials on
offer are now innovative and sophisticated. Below this well-designed
cutlery drawer are robust pull-out
drawers for frequently used crockery.

THE PRACTICAL AND THE POSSIBLE

Storage is an important concern of contemporary design. More than ever
before, the things that we use, wear, look
at, eat and drink have become an intrinsic part of our lives. Be they practical or
purely decorative items, we tend to accumulate far more than we actually need,
and because we are loathe to get rid of
the excess we are constantly searching
for ways in which to accommodate it.
Kitchens are full of clever storage techniques, as we not only need to store food
but also the equipment to cook, serve
and consume it. However, every aspect
of our homes will require some kind of
storage and it is therefore important to
consider this when making any changes
to our living space.

Good design is a combination of
practicality and aesthetics. A well
designed space is not inspiration alone –
it requires some simple calculations so
that tasks can be performed efficiently
and safely. The science of ergonomics
(how people function within a working
environment) relies on information
about the measurements of the human
body – anthropometrics. Together they
allow us to predict and ensure the practical efficiency of individual rooms.

It is not sufficient for a kitchen to look good – it must also work well. Kitchen cupboards conceal a multitude of functions behind their sophisticated veneer, from dishwasher to rubbish bin, located strategically next to each other.

Ingenious ideas for storage can equip even the smallest kitchen with sufficient room to house those space-consuming daily items that otherwise tend to languish on work surfaces.

RIGHT **The open-plan arrangement of many lofts has tended to change our attitude towards privacy and** we are now happy to reveal rather than conceal many of life's daily necessities. With so many wonderful looking gadgets and accessories available in the shops, kitchen storage has become a focus of display. Traditional cupboards are being replaced by open shelving units in eye-catching materials.

Planning is very often a matter of common sense and every environment we inhabit should be thought through to provide a coherent space. Patterns of movement need to be considered, for example, so that people can move through an area without falling over, knocking into things or constantly needing to take a circuitous route. The kitchen is an example of a task-focused space (preparing food, cooking, cleaning and washing up) where juxtapositions, levels, convenience and safety must be held in complex balance. The term 'work triangle', used to describe a physical relationship between the primary working sites in the kitchen, could usefully be applied to other regions of the house that are often left to chance. Although it is not usually thought of as personal, storage needs to relate closely to the requirements of those using the rooms on a daily basis.

EASE OF ACCESS

Probably the most important part of storage is the ability to access it. If an item is difficult and time-consuming to get out, it will either not be put away or it will not be used. We have all abandoned the struggle with an over-full,

awkwardly positioned cupboard or a drawer that is difficult to open and close. Hidden storage will succeed or fail on two levels: how well it has been practically engineered, and how well the relationship of each unit to the other units and the tasks required has been considered. Given that it is hidden, the difference between an expensive and a cheap fitting will be how well it works. It is much better to spend money on a well-designed and manufactured system and make savings on the exterior finish than the other way round.

In contrast, some storage items are obviously attractive and designed to make a pleasant addition to a room. The work surface on the right is set into a table-like unit with an open shelf underneath where equipment is stored in open aluminium catering boxes. The whole scheme is driven by the idea of practicality. No time should be wasted in looking for things in this kitchen – even the time taken to open a cupboard door has been saved. The sink is also well positioned to offer not only good light, but also a pleasant aspect to anyone washing or preparing food here.

Some objects that were once hidden away have now become attractive items in their own right. Product designers have contributed heavily to this turn in events and the visual impact of domestic items is considered as important as their ability to work efficiently. The shape and materials of individual kitchen implements, from sieves to garlic presses, frying pans to baking trays, are viewed as potential ornament and hung on wall-hugging vertical racks close to the surfaces of use. The hi-fi was traditionally hidden away in minimalist black, but the latest CD player is designed to be hung prominently on the wall.

The proportions of this attic bathroom are low and compact, in balance with the sloping ceiling. The shelf and false wall behind the bidet conceals the plumbing and echoes the oblong shape of the pair of matching vellum trunks.

Displays of personal mementoes can also enhance the character of a room. Sporting accessories, framed photographs, historical memorabilia, and military souvenirs, for example, can provide attractive wall displays, freeing up shelves for further storage. In the bathroom above, two well-used trunks are a charming complement to a light coloured bathroom, and they offer good storage for linen. They occupy an awkward space that if filled with built-in cupboards would visually reduce and

unbalance the room. Excessive storage is often a problem in bathrooms, where a cluster of cabinets can make them functional rather than relaxing spaces.

A large amount of storage space in bedrooms and bathrooms is probably best offered by built in, or made to measure, free-standing cupboards. Clearly there is an advantage to free-standing units, as they do not become part of the fabric of the house and can be carried on to the next property if required. Do not underestimate, however, the increased cost in purchasing a piece of furniture rather than having something built in.

In the bathroom below, two large cupboards have been built to fit either side of the window, offering copious storage, including a boiler and hanging space for shirts. Painted a recessive blue grey, they harmonize with the restrained, French country design. The large expanses of cupboard front have been broken up with simple fielded panels and the proportion of handles and doors has been carefully thought out. Interestingly, the units have not been built up to the ceiling but stop just short of it, giving us the feeling that the space still exists beyond each cupboard. Clearly this room is fortunate to have plenty of natural direct sunlight – even with the blind half-drawn the room is still well lit. In a different space, care should be taken in positioning units of this size, as they will considerably reduce natural light.

SHELVING AND OPEN STORAGE

Quantities of items of the same theme add character and rhythm to a room. Books are a typical example, where the shape and size of individual volumes become ingredients in a decorative

The luxury of space in a modern bathroom is relatively rare, making good storage even more important. These elegant, painted cupboards are both functional and decorative, complementing the calm, contemplative atmosphere of the room.

There is something very satisfying about a display of neat piles of beautifully ironed white shirts, rows of polished shoes and smart boxes of socks and underwear. Contrasts of colour and texture enhance the rhythm, and objects should be in proportion with the dimensions of the shelves.

pattern. For practical as well as aesthetic reasons, ensure that larger books are located on the bottom and the smallest at the top. Bookshelves are a common storage feature of many homes, often simply tucked into niches or areas of 'dead' space. Do not be afraid to experiment with shelving, however; it can be very effective in highlighting the natural curves, corners and features of a particular room. If sympathetic materials and colours are used, even a whole wall of shelves should not dominate unduly. Do not be deterred by a doorway, as shelves can be taken over the door and made into an architectural feature. Remember that details like the skirting should be carried on from the adjacent walls across the bottom of the shelves. Such small points will make all the difference to how the room accepts the shelves while retaining its integrity.

Shelving can be a way not only of storing things but also of changing the dimensions of a room. The traditional country-style shelf that runs around a kitchen is used to store and display plates as well as set up a strong horizontal line to act like a horizon. This will reduce the height and increase the feeling of lateral space, especially if the wall

is treated to a different colour above and below the shelf.

As new ingredients that need to be stored enter into our daily living space – whether they are CDs, office materials or computer software – convenient and attractive shelving becomes ever more important. Open shelving for such similar, repetitive items can be both interesting and functional, as it avoids closing off the items from the activity of the room. Clothing can also create attractive, recurring colours or shapes. Vertical layers of shirts or linen, towels or shoe boxes, can be compressed into a harmonious and contained unit, again exploiting the perspective of larger spaces and items being placed closer to the ground. The bedroom on the left displays an efficient and coherent example of open storage placed on the adjoining wall to the bathroom beyond. In this case it is a far more practical solution than cupboard doors, with the added benefit of a repeated horizontal line that helps add width to the room. For all its practicality, however, think hard about how tidy you are. You may want to incorporate additional closed storage features into your design if you know you do not have the required discipline.

KEYNOTES

- RHYTHM AND REPETITION

- PATTERN AND DISPLAY

- EASE OF ACCESS

- ERGONOMICS

- LIGHTING TO DISTRACT OR DEFINE

- MAINTAINING PROPORTION

- THE IMPORTANCE OF DETAILS

An intriguing form of open storage was adopted by Sir John Soane at the turn of the 18th and 19th centuries. In his former home in London (left), a mesmerizing arrangement of plaster casts, part of his antique collection, directs attention to the focal point of the bust on the balustrade – appropriately, a depiction of Soane himself.

Shelves and niches do not have to be full to create impact, however. Often an even greater effect may be achieved by a single object displayed in isolation, so that the purity of its own shape and composition can be observed. An interesting Japanese tradition is to store an assortment of items in a chest beneath an alcove. A different object is placed in turn alone in the alcove to illustrate its individual beauty.

Display is an art, and the combining of objects so that they work harmoniously is a secret known to very few. Sir John Soane's collection of treasures is extravagantly displayed throughout his former home, the walls presenting a gallery of busts, urns and reliefs.

MANIPULATING
SPACE

Achieving balance and harmony makes the home functional, flexible and relaxing

Sometimes a cupboard or wardrobe lacks the stature or correct proportion for a particular room. Additional height can be achieved by using the top of the cupboard to display a collection of wooden bowls and ceramics – and amusingly angled hats on stands.

BALANCE AND PROPORTION

Space is three-dimensional and we can work with it in many ways. We can adapt it for practical requirements, to store or display things, or use it inspirationally, to create structures that liberate and uplift us. Space should be enjoyed and can be used for some, if not all, of these ways at the same time. In order to get the best out of any area, we must consider the ways in which we experience it and how it was originally designed. The rules that governed and brought order to the structure when it was first designed should be understood in principle, so that we can choose whether to accommodate or challenge them.

A space that is balanced possesses a relaxing visual equilibrium that we experience as calming and beneficial.

In manipulating individual rooms, it is important to think about the fabric of the building, so that we are not creating unresolved tensions in the new look. One immediate area to consider is the relationship of vertical and horizontal lines in a room, for example window and door frames, picture edges, furniture and patterns. A successful design needs to balance the two contrasting ingredients: the horizontal line is relaxing and remote, whereas the vertical one is restraining and immediate. All rooms, in fact, contain elements of both, but a space that works aesthetically will hold the two in harmony.

Most of us will be able to see that a piece of furniture or a painting works well in a certain room but not know why. By recognizing why something looks

LEFT Rooms can be divided into different spaces by introducing certain devices. Changing flooring material, for example, whether in texture, colour or composition, will alter the atmosphere of a room. In the elegant setting, ornamental columns and an arch enhance the demarcation of the two areas.

RIGHT A uniform colour scheme which runs through several rooms can deceive the eye with a false impression of size. This is reinforced when a room is not over-furnished and the floor space is delineated by using diverse textural materials – in this case, limestone and carpet.

century chimney-piece, the depth of architrave, even within the sections of individual mouldings. Each of these elements set up invisible lines within the room that act like a grid and help us to choose and position furniture and accessories successfully. The size and shape of pieces will either conform to the ratios set within a room or clash with it.

In seeking to design and decorate rooms to their full potential, it is invaluable to know how and why decisions on the space's dimensions were originally made. New arrangement and decoration should take account of these original principles or at least be aware of how they work. Classical ideas of proportion still influence designs of today; in a modern neo-classical house, for example, ceilings may be lower and cornices narrower, but the scale and ratio of each room sets a tempo that can be recognized and developed. The deep skirtings of a high-ceilinged 19th-century room can be seen in a reduced size in the modern equivalent. The danger here is when the smaller, mass-produced skirting or architrave, which is made for the modern home, is reinstated in a period space; few mouldings conform to classical proportions and when installed often look

right or wrong, by considering its relationship with the architecture of the room, we should gain in confidence and learn to look more effectively.

Proportion has been another key feature of design since Ancient Greek and Roman times, when every part of a building was measured against the classical column and the ratio between its various elements (see page 35). Thus all parts of any one building were created in proportion and in harmony. Although we may not have any actual columns in a house, it does not mean that they have

no bearing on the initial dimensions, or are not responsible for details and their proportions. A room from the 19th century, for example, is likely to have deep skirtings, a dado rail and a cornice at the top. These decorative elements of the room all began in the classical column. Seen in cross section, the capital became the cornice, the cylindrical shaft became the wall, the plinth developed into the skirting board and so on. The same ratios that appear in different elements of a column also manifest in smaller details in the structure of a simple 19th-

We enjoy harmony, proportion and balance in our

surroundings because they are part of our nature

This ensuite bathroom is located in a niche with minimal demarcation from the rest of the room. Such openness is relatively unusual, but allows a potentially small and cramped area to enjoy the light, colours and atmosphere in the rest of the space.

KEYNOTES

- INTRODUCING SCREENS
- ESTABLISHING A HIERARCHY
- VERTICALS AND HORIZONTALS
- PROPORTION
- ADJUSTING LEVELS OF LIGHT
- CONTINUITY AND DIVISION
- FLOOR AND WALL TREATMENTS

mean and disconnected from the rest of the space. It is important to let the space tell us what it needs, and to understand that the shell of the classically inspired building will dictate what will look right, down to each detail.

DIVIDING UP SPACE

In most traditional homes, rooms are adjacent to one another and each has a clearly defined function, decoration and atmosphere. However, in order to create a complete and unified scheme we need to ensure that some continuity runs through these individual spaces. The modern setting on page 65 offers a very strong element of unity. Once we have entered the first space from the hallway, all the spaces beyond are treated with the same flooring and appear as one flowing space. They have been opened up rather than subdivided, and as such work in a way not dissimilar to when they were first built. Although the proportions of this space imply a classical structure, the room has been treated in a minimalist way. The full-height screens that hang from a recessed track seem to float above the crisp, cool flooring, contrasting with the anchoring circular stones that point into the room. We can

see that beyond the first screen there is a further screen that is closed, giving the feeling that the space infinitely extends. These sliding screens allow the space to feel dynamic, not static, and to work with much more flexibility. They do need to be carefully planned in, however, so that they slide into a convenient parking position when not in use.

Before dividing a room, consider the volume of the room in its simplest form. We need to question whether the subdivision of this singular room will benefit the two new spaces or provide us with two awkward shapes. The more permanent a division, the more impact on the space. The division of a room does not have to be opaque. It may take the form of a free-standing screen of columns instead of a wall, which will allow views of the combined area from either side of the screen at all times (see page 64). Although there is a demarcation, the regions are not completely separate. Such a connected space is acoustically and psychologically very different to that of two separated rooms. More flexible screening devices include pieces of furniture, plants and panels of fabric. These all change the dimensions of the room and offer a certain privacy to each area.

The subtlest spatial division may be merely implied with a change of floor level or a contrast in surface treatment or texture. Such a division, used in the living room above, can be read as a single volume of space which has been divided into zones. This allows an even greater degree of flexibility, and results in a more open and light feeling across the zoned areas. The arrangement of furniture helps to underline the diverse moods of one space and another. This well adjusted room shows a clear division in which two spaces work together harmoniously. The active dining area in the foreground contains hard, practical surfaces that will encourage noise and chatter. Beyond is the quieter, more relaxing part, with a light coloured, sound absorbing rug precisely distinguishing one space from the other. An attractive sense of stillness is achieved by arranging the furniture in the sitting area symmetrically. Light is diffused through an opaque blind to give an air of oriental harmony, reinforced by the flower arrangements and sparse furnishing used throughout the room.

The tradition of living/dining rooms has been given a new, contemporary emphasis in this sensitive demarcation of space. A skilful use of light, colour and textural contrast has resulted in two clearly distinct yet unified environments, each suited to their individual purpose.

A SUMMARY OF **THE ESSENTIALS**

An interior design has to make visual sense of the relationship between you, your belongings, your family and how you live.

BALANCE

PROPORTION

HIERARCHY

FORM

SYMMETRY

PERSPECTIVE

ORDER

SIMPLICITY

RHYTHM

HARMONY

2

LIGHT

Light is one of the least understood aspects of design, yet daylight and artificial illumination are essential to our perceptions of a room. The flexibility of modern lighting techniques allows us to appreciate and inhabit a space as well as giving it colour, atmosphere and impact. Natural light can also be softened and coloured through fabric window treatments and a range of textured surfaces. Through a balance of ambient, task and accent lighting, and a careful selection of curtains, blinds, fittings, switches and shades, we can create a design that works at any time or occasion.

LEFT Imaginatively designed pendulum lights bring a decorative focus to this clean, reflective space.

THE IMPACT OF LIGHT

Light defines space and creates atmosphere in a room, and the balance of different sources determines its success

RIGHT A tranquil corner of this drawing room benefits from the natural light spilling through the tall French windows. The light is reflected further into the room by the ornately framed mirror, giving it an open and airy feel.

CHANGING COLOUR AND SPACE

The different ways of perceiving space can be influenced and controlled. A clever lighting scheme will modify the way in which we view a particular room and respond to its individual style or look. Whether natural or artificial, light changes how we view textures, colours and shapes. It can radically shift the emphasis from one area of a room to another through a careful balance of different sources. Light is a highly effective tool to highlight a room's assets and distract from its weaknesses, and it also shapes the overall mood.

The way in which patterns of light and shade are created can change how we regard even everyday objects. On the right, for example, a simple Venetian blind is transformed by four low-voltage, recessed downlighters. In the sitting room opposite, the natural light streaming in through the window controls the room's perceived depth. The *chaise-longue* is thrown into relief, and the reflective floor enhances the effect by picking up the shape of its legs in silhouette. Light can divide a large room by focusing on a specific area – a dining area, say – whilst leaving the rest of a space in semi-darkness. Subdued light

from lamps and candles can create intimate pockets of light, while general lighting can extend a sense of space. Combined with mirrors and reflective surfaces, it can make a room appear significantly larger than it is. 'Washing' walls with an even layer of light can also be used to expand the apparent area (see page 95). If the wall is light in colour, the effect of this technique is even greater.

ABOVE Downlighters above this kitchen sink cast pools of light on the surrounding work surface, while during the daytime the area will be flooded with natural light filtering through the Venetian blind.

LEFT **Entrance halls have a tendency to be dark. Architectural details, such as fanlights or** strategically placed windows around the door itself, can direct additional light deep into the interior of the house.

RIGHT **Gloss paint on the floor provides an additional reflective surface to enhance the effect of** the light pouring through the large windows of this converted 19th-century schoolhouse. Contemporary hanging and standard lamps show how imaginative lighting effects will be achieved at night.

The shape and features of a room can be accentuated by using directed and specific light sources, whereas low, uniform light will make features fade into the background. High-lit curved walls or stairs can bring a sense of movement into a static room and uplighters, or well-placed spotlights, can profile beamed or decorative ceilings. The angle at which light strikes individual objects will also influence the appearance of dramatic shapes and features. Surface textures of walls, floors, furnishings and ornaments also respond to light in varying ways, either being thrown into relief or flattened according to the angle and intensity of the light source.

Clever lighting can also improve the appearance of very narrow rooms such as hallways, landings or corridors. The

SWITCHING ON WITH BULBS

Standard light bulbs, of the type we are most familiar with, are incandescent lamps. They create light by passing an electric current through a wire coil until it becomes luminous. This type of bulb, however, wastes a lot of energy through heat, and there are many other options in modern lighting design.

Discharge lamps pass an electric current through gases or metallic vapours in a bulb. This produces a fluorescent discharge, which passes through the phosphor coating inside the bulb or tube to become visible as light. Very energy-efficient at high pressure, they generate less heat than incandescent lamps.

Fluorescent tubes use the same mechanism as discharge lamps, but operate at lower pressures. The bulbs can contain different mixtures of gases and therefore produce different coloured light – usually slightly blue in tone, which has the cool appearance of summer daylight. New designs of fluorescent lamps work well in the home, especially where a flat wash-light is needed. Compact fluorescent tubes use the same method, but the source of light is smaller and therefore more controllable. Miniature fluorescent tubes are available that produce light as strong as a conventional lamp.

Low voltage tungsten halogen lamps, the most efficient form of incandescent lamp, produce a more neutral or white light and therefore show colours more truthfully. Low voltage lamps are smaller and easier to direct, more economic and produce a very precise light. Tungsten halogen lamps need a transformer to reduce the voltage, which can be dimmed through a special switch.

GLS lamps, or standard light bulbs, produce red-yellow light. They enhance the tone of warm colours, such as red and orange, but dull blues and greens. The quality of light is much lower than low-voltage tungsten.

When natural light is not readily available, using the space to good advantage is vital in order to achieve a light and airy atmosphere. Artificial light is carefully placed in this kitchen, and the pale and smooth surfaces reflect it back around the space.

will also influence the room's mood. Different types of light sources give different coloured 'white' light and it is therefore vital to consider the type of light a lamp produces when you start to develop a lighting scheme.

Not only its colour quality, but also its intensity play a major role in light's effect on a space. The extent to which light varies in brightness, depending on the time of day, weather conditions and location, is amazing. While dependable brightness from natural light cannot be guaranteed, artificial light will produce a consistent brightness that can be conveniently controlled.

The side effect of brightness is glare. This may be the result of harsh sunlight, an unshaded lamp or excessive contrast between lit areas and those in shadow. Described as either direct or reflected, glare can be tiring to the eyes and care should be taken to avoid it, particularly in a relaxed, comfortable environment.

The opposite of glare is blandness. This effect is created when every part of a room is equally bright. A space lit in this way will appear dull, whereas a balance of high and low light keeps us alert and interested. When it appears in a small, contained area, glare may be con-

placing of lights along shorter walls will draw the eye away from the long walls so that the room appears wider than it actually is. Lighting can also be used to encourage the movement of people in a dynamic area by defining the chosen route with higher lighting levels.

PROPERTIES OF LIGHT

Our perceptions of colour are totally dependent on light. Without light, colour would not exist, because what our brains translate as colour is the reflected hue from light falling on an

object. When we split uncoloured or 'white' light by shining it through a glass prism, we realize that this colourless light actually contains all the colours of the spectrum. Even in its undivided form, what we take to be white light is rarely pure. Rather, it will have a slightly red/yellow bias, which gives it a warm tone, or a blue/green bias that will characterize the light as being cool. Because true colour quality is only revealed by pure white light, this cool or warm white light will affect the clarity of colours within a room scheme. As such it

The unusual shape of the window in this German barn dominates the room and is highlighted by the mixture of coloured strip lights and spots dotted around the ceiling. The isolated group of chairs is almost silhouetted against the blank canvas of the window.

strued as sparkle – the glitter of light from a chandelier or cut glass and the twinkling of burning candles. These visible light sources or reflections serve as delicate highlights within a room and contribute to a mood of celebration and play. Starlights – small halogen capsules with no shade or reflector – can be fitted on the ceiling to produce similarly fine, bright sources of light.

DEFINING ATMOSPHERE

Because light has a direct effect on the emotions, the characteristics of a light source can sometimes have an unexpected effect on the atmosphere of a room. A cool, bluish light, for example, will create a serene, focused atmosphere. A red-orange light stimulates a warmer, more intimate setting, giving rise to the cliché of candles and firelight. It is important to allow for changes of mood even in functional areas, and in doing so exploit fully the flexibility of modern lighting techniques. The kitchen cum dining room on the left, for example, is lit by low-voltage downlighters, which are on a circuit controlled by dimmers.

The kitchen area contains narrow beam fittings that provide a scalloped pattern across the cupboards. The lights in the dining area have been dimmed for the softer atmosphere created by the glow of candles and some reflective sparkle from the metal pots.

Although less under our control, variations in natural light will also affect a space and the appearance of objects and colours within it. Midday sun, the source of light nearest to pure white light, can be harsh and unforgiving and tends to flatten a setting. Warm, late afternoon sunlight, on the other hand, softens hard edges, and its complex shadows give depth to a space. This fluctuation is particularly important in rooms that are dominated by natural light.

DESIGNING WITH LIGHT

All lighting design, however complex, is based on three key elements: general, ambient lighting for everyday illumination; task lighting for local, specific activities; and accent lighting to highlight particular objects or areas. All three elements need to be balanced carefully in a room, keeping its functions and atmosphere in mind.

General lighting may use either direct sources – recessed or track ceiling fixtures, for example – or indirect sources, such as lights concealed in cornices or wall-mounted uplighters. These will provide a reasonably consistent light level throughout the space. Task lighting, as its name implies, provides particular activities with concentrated light. Light-

A stainless steel kitchen provides a multitude of reflective surfaces that bounce and increase light. Glasses displayed on shelves above a granite worktop add to the effect of a room drenched in white light.

ing part of a living room used as a home office, kitchen work surfaces or a bedroom for reading are typical examples.

It is a good idea to try to position task lighting in a way that does not cast shadows or glare on the work that is being lit. The task lighting in the sleek, contemporary kitchen on the left is very effective: light sources are positioned just above the surface, between the hand and the eye of the person performing the task. Accent lighting provided higher up creates a stimulating reflection and sparkle.

Accent lighting focuses illumination on a specific object, area or feature in a room. This is often done by using a key light to profile an object with a single point of light. This creates strong highlights and shadows, and increases the impact of both the object's contours and texture. The precise effect that is

achieved depends on the angle of the beam and on its intensity.

Accent lighting can also be used to emphasize the shape of a space, or to fool the eye into believing that it is either larger or a different shape. Remember to allow for as much flexibility as possible, using different types of lamp and dimmer systems to create a variety of looks or moods at different times of the day.

The cleverly lit kitchen illustrated below uses colour to accent the recesses on either side of the hob. A cool blue fluorescent light source within each recess, probably incorporating a blue/green filter, complements the warm wooden tones of the furniture. The overall effect succeeds because a number of different circuits can be turned up or down in order to achieve this balance of light in a well used, versatile room.

KEYNOTES

- INTERPLAY OF LIGHT AND SHADOW
- DEFINING A FOCAL POINT
- HIGHLIGHTING COLOUR
- FLEXIBILITY AND CONTROL
- EMPHASIZING TEXTURE
- LOCAL AND SPECIFIC LIGHT
- DIRECT AND INDIRECT SOURCES

The kitchen is probably the most complicated and demanding room in the home to light successfully. Its combination of daily activities requires a wide variety of lighting – bright, directional light for cooking and food preparation, pools of light over the table and downlighters for display cabinets and kitchen units.

MAXIMIZING
NATURAL LIGHT

A home bathed in natural daylight is a great pleasure,
but it still has to be tailored to the needs of a room

THE CHARACTER OF NATURAL LIGHT

Most modern buildings are designed to accommodate our desire for a plentiful amount of daylight, now acknowledged to have physical and psychological benefits. Obtaining sufficient light may be more of a problem in period homes with fewer windows and smaller panes, but a successful interior should still maximize the level and quality of natural light and control its effects.

A room can receive natural light in a number of ways. It can be directly lit by sunlight, filled with reflected light from facing buildings or bathed with light filtered through gardens and vegetation. Both the rooms illustrated here contain an abundance of natural light that floods the space. Situated on upper floors of buildings, they remain naturally lit for longer than most rooms. The voile dressings at both sets of windows serve to reduce the glare from direct sunlight, which may be very intense, particularly at midday.

The direction in which a room faces and the times of year will determine both the quantity and quality of light it receives, and it is important to consider this before allocating particular tasks to specific rooms. Generally speaking, north light is cool and steady and casts few shadows; as a result, artists favour both its clarity and constancy in a focused working space. East light is morning light that decreases in brightness as the day develops; kitchens and bedrooms often benefit from strong morning light at the time when they are most used. South light is a warm light that constantly shifts during the day and which needs to be tempered in summer to reduce high room temperatures and glare. West light can be warm and rich in

Natural light needs to be controlled in much the same way as artificial light to avoid glare or shadow distorting a room's design. Too much light through large windows can significantly change its subtle decoration, and the introduction of sheers acts as a diffuser, filtering and softening the daylight.

Placing a *chaise longue* or a table against a large window can help to take a little of the surplus light away from the room. It also produces some interesting shapes and silhouettes, as well as reflections from the highly polished floor.

the late afternoon, although its brightness may sometimes be overpowering, especially with a low winter sun.

Natural light also changes in quantity and quality with latitude, which in turn influences the colours that work best in different parts of the world. This explains why that brightly coloured painting you brought back from the Caribbean does not look as good in Britain, and why terracotta never looks the same in Mediterranean countries as it does in Britain. In such areas of steady, high quality natural light, the strong, mellow daylight enlivens clear pastels, strong hues and rich colours. Muted decorating colours tend to be chosen in mid-northern Europe because of its low quality natural light – a soft, grey/blue. This is why in Scandinavia pure green, blues and pinks are used to brighten up the short days of winter.

Light can be used to create contrast in a design. The dark work surfaces and pale wooden units in this sophisticated kitchen/dining room work well within the light space with its high ceilings.

KEYNOTES

- CONSIDERING ASPECT

- AVOIDING CONTRAST AND GLARE

- REFLECTING AND FILTERING LIGHT

- SKYLIGHTS AND BLINDS

- TINTING GLASS IN SUNLIGHT

- COLOURING NATURAL LIGHT

- WINDOW TREATMENTS

WORKING WITH NATURAL LIGHT

Obviously, the easiest way to maximize available daylight is to use large openings, such as clear glass windows or skylights. However, while the size of a window or skylight is regulated by many factors – the construction of the walls or ceiling, the need for privacy, the view and necessary ventilation, for example – the location and orientation of a window or skylight is far more important in determining the quality of daylight a room receives.

Very bright light creates a sharp contrast between light and shadow. It also clearly highlights individual shapes and colours, apparent even through drawn, translucent curtains. Indirect light, by contrast, remains fairly constant, softening the harshness of direct sunlight and balancing the light level within a space. A carefully positioned skylight will capture this ambient and diffuse light throughout the day, as will other openings oriented away from direct sunlight.

Direct sunshine needs to be controlled, reflected and softened to avoid glare and excessive contrast. Much of its energy is received by us as heat, and strong light can create almost unbearable temperatures in a south-facing

room in summer. The high-ceilinged kitchen cum dining room illustrated on the left, for example, has a large wall of glass that faces north; it thus receives reflected light, which is useful for a working space. The high roof-light provides good top light to illuminate deeper parts of the room, while the highly reflective surfaces of chairs, table, work surfaces and handles all contribute to its overall light level.

The most effective way to control natural light levels is by using reflected light, because each time daylight is reflected from a surface it is spread and softened. This reduces light intensity and evens out brightness and contrasts, thus improving the quality of light and general visibility. If, as in this kitchen, a window is positioned along the edge of a wall or at the corner of a room, daylight will 'wash' the surface of the adjacent wall. It becomes an illuminated surface and itself a source of light within a space.

Light can also be reflected before it enters the room, using louvres and blinds, or by filtering it outside through trees, shrubs or vines. Horizontal louvres of the sort that make up a Venetian blind control light effectively, as they can be adjusted according to conditions.

If a room is permanently suffused with light, the design of flexible blinds or curtains should take this into account. On the left, transparent blinds screen the top half of the windows, ensuring a gentler, lower light source into the room. On the right, sheer curtains screen the view in and out of a city bathroom.

Such louvres can reflect ground light from outside by bouncing it towards the ceiling and deep into the interior of large rooms. Alternatively, they can direct high-level light towards opposite walls or towards the floor.

The most efficient way of reducing the build up of heat from solar energy is to position louvres on the outside of the glass rather than on the inside. Most Mediterranean countries have shutters for this very reason. Any build up of heat that takes place between the louvres and the glass therefore remains outside rather than inside the room.

When relying on natural foliage outside to reflect daylight, it is important to remember that the seasons will change the amount of protection offered. A room may be bathed in light on a bright winter's day, but kept in darkness during the summer when the surrounding trees are in full leaf.

DRESSING WINDOWS

Curtains or blinds can be effective in manipulating the effects of sunlight. The weave and reflectivity of the fabric determines the level of control, from creating a complete blackout to simply removing glare. You can achieve more flexibility by having two separately tracked curtains over the same opening to adapt to the light.

The cool, constant light in the living room above is reflected off an adjacent building and has its glare removed by the half-drawn cotton blinds. The small conifers that stand in pots outside the windows add their own coolness and architectural accent to the room. The contrasting atmospheres apparent in this space and in the bathroom bathed in morning sunlight opposite reveal the variable impact of natural light upon inside space.

Another way to control sunlight is to use different glazing materials or applied films. The most widely used materials for reducing solar energy are tinted glasses and plastics, but these may have a negative effect on the overall design. Glazing materials treated with metal oxides, for example, reflect light and reduce the views from outside during the day. However, in the evening they produce the opposite effect, reducing views outside while putting the interior on display. This is an aspect that should be carefully thought through. Net curtains or voiles, as well as opaque or treated glass, will obscure a view into a space only when the light levels outside are higher than those on the inside. When the sun goes down and you switch the light on, any privacy offered to the space during the day has gone. The effect of the obscured glass is reversed.

Selectively transmitting materials allow the passage of some parts of the light spectrum, while reflecting or absorbing others. The contemporary room on page 88 has one solution: it covers a large window with a panel of translucent fabric that fits neatly into the window frame. This simple technique has effectively removed the glare, but also blocked off the outside view. Such a treatment is more appropriate in an urban context, where it can provide privacy from adjacent buildings.

It is surprising how much light a room can lose when the window is dressed. It is worth considering versatile window treatments that can be adapted to accommodate different levels of light, at various times of year. The amount of light from an undressed window is apparent in the bedroom overleaf. The clean lines of the window help to give a feeling of space to the room, and its clarity is enhanced by the non-filtered light. Remember, too, that curtains are a mat-

LEFT **The subdued and controlled ambient light in this Italian architect's living room is produced by a** panel of opaque fabric. It enhances the impact of the different textures that shape the austere design.

RIGHT **A small wooden bed is positioned in a corner to benefit from the light entering by windows on** two sides. Its placement also means that the bed's occupant cannot be seen through the windows, so there is no particular need for curtains.

BELOW **For those averse to the idea of curtains, shutters are a convenient and practical alternative.** Designers use them in both contemporary and traditional schemes to provide useful security, as well as an uncluttered window treatment.

ter of personal preference rather than an essential; not everyone requires a total, or even a partial, blackout at night.

Internal, hinged shutters from the 19th century that unfold from the sides or slide across from the wall cavity at the sides or below, and slick, contemporary hinged or sliding opaque perspex sheeting, offer a very adaptable form of blackout that can be tailored to almost any setting. The hard edges of the white shutters in the dining room on the left-define and bring authority to the window area, and they also increase the available light in the room. They are suitable for a fairly formal room, but in other contexts, a room with shutters and no fabric screen at the window may seem austere. It may then be neccessary to soften the window shape to make the space more comfortable and reduce the potential for echo.

ARTIFICIAL
LIGHT

Balancing the different types of lighting is
essential in a practical and versatile design

BALANCING LIGHT

Even a space with plenty of natural light will at some point require artificial lighting. And as we increasingly use rooms for more than one purpose, the flexibility of lighting schemes will become a prime consideration. We may wish to distinguish between various areas of a room, give definition to particular features and experiment with different light sources. A balance of lighting elements enables us to create diverse effects and moods within the same space.

When you are planning a lighting scheme, it is important to bear in mind how the different parts work together. General or ambient lighting, which supplies the room's overall illumination, can be achieved by most light fixtures, including standard lamps, central pendant lamps and uplighters. Both direct and indirect sources of light can be used. While the former tends to create a great deal of glare and shadow, the latter, which has been reflected back into the room from a wall or other surface, produces much less. A combination of the two creates layers within an overall design, giving depth and interest.

Accent lighting, which is used to emphasize individual features within a

room, should exist independently from the main illumination. Many of the most recent developments in lighting – especially of new types of bulb (see page 77) – are concerned with accent lighting. In the dramatically lit corridor on the right, for example, recessed, low-voltage halogen uplighters in the foreground highlight the orchids and wash the textured wall in a glow of light. Further recessed halogens light each stair and set up an intriguing rhythm that continues into the space beyond the steps. These elements all provide direct light and are

balanced by the focal point of the light on the far wall, which produces complementary reflected light. Throughout this area, the techniques of 'washing' and 'grazing' with light to enhance the texture and shape of individual surfaces make the most of shadow and glare to introduce a sense of mystery into an otherwise difficult perspective.

Task lighting, although by definition functional, can play an important part in a decorative scheme. Although designed to illuminate local areas, many fixtures also produce more indirect light, contributing to the ambient lighting of the room. In recent years, an increased demand for light fittings that perform particular tasks has resulted in major innovations in design. We have managed to create much smaller light sources, for example, which are easier to conceal, reduce the risk of glare and have beams that are easier to direct. This is invaluable when lighting a computer desk, where it is important to keep light off the screen itself and direct it instead to the working area around.

Mirrors also need to be lit with care. So often they are lit directly, which renders them useless by causing surface glare. A more satisfactory result is gained

LEFT The low, tented ceiling of this dressing room makes it awkward to provide adequate artificial light. The lamps on the chest of drawers highlight the corners and pendant lamps are directed towards the wardrobe shelves.

RIGHT Natural and artificial light are combined in this Japanese-style bedroom. Directional lamps are concentrated around the head of the bed while diffused daylight filters through the paper screen against the window.

ABOVE Switches are not only the means of achieving varied lighting schemes. They can be decorative details in their own right, providing an opportunity to introduce a different texture and material into the room.

by crossing beams in front of the mirror to illuminate each side of the face, cancelling out the shadows.

SELECTING FITTINGS

More than any other interior device, lighting can bring an imaginative feel to the most ordinary room. Although individual preference dictates the amount and type of light required in a room, there is now such a wide variety of light fixtures that a few key factors will help you to select the most appropriate. First, try to establish what the light is meant to achieve, how it will work with other parts of the design and how often it is likely to be turned on. Then consider the style of the rest of the scheme and how the fitting can best complement it. Only then should considerations such as shape and colour come into play.

Most of the time we tend to tackle these requirements the wrong way round. The last two factors here are normally considered first, and the first and most important issue is often not even considered at all.

The most traditional form of lighting is the pendant lamp, a ceiling fitting usually placed in the centre of the room. Compared to more modern light fittings, pendant lights give an inadequate, unflattering, general light that often leaves the edges of a room in shadow. That said, they can be modified with fittings and shades to improve the light produced and to reduce their glare. Two pendant lamps of standard opal incandescent bulbs, for example, provide a warm yellow general light to the tented dressing room opposite. Accent and interest is provided by the two table

lamps that also contain standard incandescent bulbs. Silk shades both reduce the glare and funnel the light up and down from the bulbs. They draw you in by lighting both the focal point – the hats – and the ceiling fabric above.

Uplighters, as their name suggests, throw their beam upwards to reflect off walls and ceilings and provide soft, indirect lighting. They can be wall-mounted, free-standing or recessed, with a consequent effect upon the light produced.

Position, and the texture and reflective quality of the illuminated surface, also influence the final result. Although they can produce glare, uplighters can provide good general lighting or some imaginative effects. In a relatively large space, uplighters can be used to increase awareness of the dimensions of a room and to highlight ceiling designs or grand cornices. On a smaller scale, a free-standing uplighter placed behind an object can be used to backlight and cast

The buttresses against the wall of this modern library create niches for a pair of slim standard lamps. Positioned behind matching cream armchairs, they provide ideal task lighting for reading or other study.

interesting shadows within a space. This is particularly effective with architectural plants or flowers, as in the relatively dark corner illustrated on the right. In this room, much of the general light is absorbed by the combination of dark furniture, heavily framed pictures and patterned fabric. However, what might have been a problem is made a virtue by the dramatic backlighting of the vase, which is enhanced by the low light levels in the rest of the room.

Table and standard lamps are useful, flexible sources of either task or general lighting (see page 105). The sitting room on the left is a naturally light space; two armchairs complement the contemporary decoration and draw on a cream palette to reflect the light even more. The symmetrically placed standard lamps provide key accents and highlight the thrust of the vertical piers. As they come in all shapes, styles and sizes, standard lamps can complement an existing design scheme, mixed and matched with appropriate shades and bases. When selecting stands and bases separately, make sure that their size, style and colour are balanced.

Wall lights are another traditional source of general or background light-

ing. Like pendant lights, traditional fittings can produce glare, although many modern designs avoid or reduce this. Conventional picture lights are a form of wall-mounted accent lighting, and at night, together with low-level general lighting, they can produce a subtle, relaxing effect.

Wall 'washers' are an innovative form of downlighter (or possibly uplighter) that create an 'airy' impression, pushing the walls out to give a feeling of greater space. Depending on the beam's angle, wall washing can produce a subtle glow or accentuate paintings or ornamental features. The orientally inspired bedroom shown on the previous page, for example, is washed by the cool natural light that floods in through the opaque screen wall. A general light is given by the fluorescent tubes above the bed head that light the three panels; because they are baffled, they create a diffused light that gently washes the wall. Two narrow beamed, recessed halogen downlights in the same bulkhead are used as low-voltage accent lights. This results in a soft, restful pool of light on each pillow.

Downlighting is obviously the reverse of uplighting. Lamps can be recessed in the ceiling, fitted on a suspended track,

KEYNOTES

- DIRECTING LIGHT

- HIGHLIGHTING TEXTURE

- ELIMINATING SHADOW

- COMBINING SOURCES OF LIGHT

- GENERAL, TASK, ACCENT LIGHT

- WALLWASHING TECHNIQUES

- LAMP FITTINGS AND BULBS

wall-mounted or even free standing. If used independently from other light sources, they can make a ceiling appear lower and darker and can cause glare. Some low-voltage downlight systems offer extra flexibility by suspending any number of lamps along a length of cable under tension. Downlighters can also be used very effectively to cast pools of light at floor level, and to bring texture and depth to rooms with limited dimensions.

Downlighting can combine practical and dramatic effects. The two orchids illuminated here are cleverly downlit by recessed, low-voltage lamps in each alcove. The full needs of the space have been borne in mind, as there is sufficient reflected light from the walls to illuminate a face at the mirror without shadow.

Bathrooms are often located in areas where there is no natural light, so good artificial lighting is therefore very important. Often mirrored walls and other reflective surfaces are incorporated to increase a room's apparent size, and recessed downlighters in the ceiling can throw a generous arc of light around the room.

PLAYING WITH LIGHT

Nothing tricks the eye as successfully as light, and it is therefore the delight of the decorative illusionist

In the days before electricity, mirrors were often used to enhance candle, oil or gas light in a room. They might be placed in dark corners or close to windows, and the bevelled, multi-faceted glass, often with an ornamental glass frame, created diverting reflections.

SETTING THE SCENE

Natural lighting in a room never remains constant for long, because it will always be subject to the changing position of the sun, the patterns of light and shade and the impact of foliage and clouds. The range of artificial lighting now available means that even without daylight we can achieve the same varied effects by manipulating different sources of light in a room. We can use techniques of illumination to tease or divert, impress or reassure, adapting the mood as required over a period of time. Modern lighting schemes enable us all to create our own theatres of public or private engagement, in which we can direct the atmosphere on each individual stage.

THE ART OF REFLECTION

Mirrors are a key element in creating the tricks and illusions of many intriguing lighting schemes. Their impact on our sense of perspective, and the level of both artificial and natural lighting in an inside space, is considerable. Strategic positioning of a looking glass on a wall adjacent to that of a window or opening will reflect more light back into the room. On a smaller scale, wall sconces will do the same with flickering candle-light. A series of reflections angled in relation to one another creates a domestic hall of mirrors, in which illusion and reality become intertwined. The triptych of glass on the dressing table above, for example, bounces images of the candle-

Apart from being extremely decorative, mirrors can also create
balance in a room. This beautiful
glass in its mirrored frame is placed
above the small 19th-century fireplace. It introduces a note of
grandeur and harmonious proportion to the attic bedroom.

has worn away over the years, produce
soft, cloudy, imperfect images that can
give a gentle air to a room. Paint can also
soften a mirror's impact, and etched
images worked onto the glass can distract attention from the image itself. Soft
artificial lighting, such as candlelight, is
very attractive when reflected; it echoes
the tradition of votive lamps in shrines
and brings the stimulus of continual
movement into a room. Humorous lighting ideas, such as the flexible, snake-like
floor illumination on page 102, also
work well when reflected, doubling the
sense of fun in an imaginative scheme.

THE MAGIC OF COLOURED LIGHT

Skilful combinations of colour and light
can be pure theatre, dominating a room
with their boldness or providing a
discreet, local change in atmosphere to
one particular area. Wall 'washing',
where light is projected over the surface
of a wall, or 'grazing' – placing a light
source very close to the wall to highlight
its textural variation – can turn a
functional wall into the key feature of a
room and magically transform our sense
of the overall space. Stained glass is
highly responsive to both daylight and
artificial light; its use in religious
traditions illustrates its ability to create
an atmosphere beyond that of the
everyday world. In the glorious Gothic
cathedral at Chartres, for example, the
blues and reds of its magnificent
windows create a beautifully soft,

Mirrors are also useful in rooms
without any other ornamentation.
In this all white bedroom, the huge
mirror becomes a design feature. It
establishes a defined focal point
which compensates for the absence
of pictures, plants and other items.

stick and vase back and forth in a dizzy-
ing visual echo.

Reflections from mirrors can actually
completely reinterpret a space. The
ornate, down-tilted mirror above carries
an alternative glimpse of the view from
the window on the adjacent wall, while
its mirrored frame brings as much light
as possible into the room. Dominating
the room with its wide frame, the
upward tilt of the full-length glass on the
left reflects back into the room both the
light from the window and that of the
recessed ceiling lights. This mirror provides a key focal point and sets up an
axis (see page 32) in the room.

Glass is a very versatile material, and
the tone of the light it reflects can vary
widely. Antique mirrors, whose silvering

In Frank Lloyd Wright's own study at Oak Park, Illinois, light filtering through the stained glass windows is complemented by the green glass shades on a pair of pendant lamps in one corner. Coloured glass shades can provide an interesting change of focus and mood.

The four storeys of this London mews house are linked by an open-plan, whitewashed staircase that leads up from a tiled courtyard on the ground floor. Tall palm trees reach up through the building, flourishing under a large skylight that bounces patterns of light off the white walls.

diffused, violet light that has an unearthly glimmer. In a domestic setting, stained glass has long been a traditional feature of 'crossroad' areas such as halls and front doors, where the changing patterns it produces can be observed throughout the day. The famous American architect Frank Lloyd Wright introduced jewel-like chips of coloured glass into the window and skylight of his study, illustrated on the preceding page. The majority of the light in this space is filtered through geometric coloured glass, bringing a comfortable softness to the rather square and linear room.

BALANCING LIGHT AND SPACE

Light wells are a response to our need to bring natural light into the centre of a building, from where it can radiate outwards into other rooms. The idea

extends back thousands of years – the famous British architect Sir John Soane (see page 23) built large light wells into his house in London, bringing light down from the roof level into the crypt below. He also used mirrors to draw light down and into dark interior spaces: placed outside the window, they were angled to catch and reflect the sky into the room below.

The dramatic stairwell pictured here is also used as a means of bringing light to the different levels of the building. The palms strengthen the close association of the space with the airy exterior world, whilst also underscoring the relationship between the different levels and introducing interesting textures and shadows to the space. The balance of light and space is quite complex; as the stairs flow downwards,

the light is reduced, requiring artificial lighting at the lower levels. At night, however, powerful uplighters could illuminate the space in reverse, throwing light up through the palms to cast fantastic shadows onto the curved stairwell walls.

The reversal of light and dark areas can be achieved by manipulating the same plane, too. Overleaf, an elaborate game surrounds the lighting of the tall bedroom and separate bathroom, which has no outside light. A large window of slightly smoked glass makes the bathroom disappear when the lights inside it are turned off, and only the bedroom is reflected in the glass. When the light levels are reversed and only the bathroom is lit, its side of the glass becomes a mirror and the bedroom beyond, in turn, temporarily vanishes.

KEYNOTES

- REFLECTION AND ILLUSION

- COLOURED GLASS

- SHADOW PLAY

- COMPLEMENTING LIGHT LEVELS

- FLEXIBILITY AND CONTROL

- DIRECTING LIGHT

- CHANGING PERSPECTIVE

LEFT Lighting can be theatrical as well as practical and small bulbs in thin transparent plastic tubing can be used to 'paint' a room with light. Here they snake across the floor, but they could equally be draped around furniture or hung across doorways and windows.

BELOW The architect of this bedroom and bathroom has ingeniously incorporated a large partition window between the two rooms. Not only is it a compact use of space, but the bathroom also benefits from the natural light filtering in through the bedroom window.

DETAILS OF LIGHTING DESIGN

*Bulbs and starlights, holders and shades, old lamps
and candles – all have a decorative part to play*

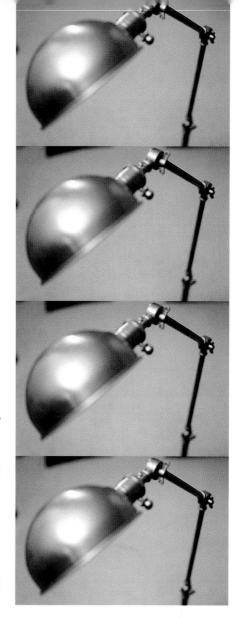

The shape, style and variety of
lamps available is overwhelming,
so choosing the right ones for your
purpose and design is an important
decision. Anglepoise lamps on flexible stems are popular as uplighters
or downlighters; they are even used
to bounce light indirectly off a
reflective surface.

CONTROLLING LIGHT

To establish a successful lighting design,
you need to understand not only the
types of lighting you need – and where –
and the fittings that are available, but
also the contribution made by bulbs and
switches. The versatility allowed by
recent developments in this field means
that now even the most difficult space
can be transformed.

Part of the flexibility offered by new
techniques is the ability to determine the
amount of light we require in specific
areas of the same room. This is particularly useful as we now seek to use light as
a medium to help us maximize available
space. A living room may accommodate
a home office or a kitchen provide the
home's main eating and social area.
Some initial calculations, based on the
activities in each part, are a useful start-
ing-point. One method for planning
light levels involves adding up the
amount of light produced by all the
bulbs in a certain space. Designers measure it in lumens (one lumen originally
being based on the quantity of light
emitted by one candle). As a general
rule, the most difficult tasks require at
least 2,500 lumens in an average room,
with the greatest number of lumens concentrated at the work location. For close,
precise work, a task lamp that provides
2,250 lumens near the work area may be
required; lower level surrounding light is
useful to minimize excessive contrast
with the rest of the room. If an area has a
more general use, 1,500 to 2,000 lumens
may be all that is required. At the
moment, many lighting designers are
working to reduce the general brightness
of rooms and to focus upon bright lighting in key task areas. This not only
encourages the conservation of energy,
but also moves away from uniform
brightness, which can be more tiring and
less interesting.

Much of the way we choose to control
light is based on the relationship
between bulb and shade. The most
important element, the quality of light, is
generated by the bulb, and it is then diffused and/or reflected by the shade. The
bulb determines the amount, direction
and colour of the light produced, whilst
the shape and size of the shade influences how the light will radiate into the
room. A coolie shade, for example,
directs the majority of the light down-
ward, and only a little upward.

A standard light bulb radiates light in
all directions from its core. If the bulb is

Table lamps play an integral part in the overall decorative impression of a room. Their size, location and juxtaposition with other objects and ornaments provide accents to give a room its individuality. The diverse shades reveal the different ways in which table lamps can influence a lighting scheme.

clear, the filament is visible and when switched on will produce maximum light – but also maximum glare. Dramatic light can be harnessed by reflecting it upwards and downwards using a card lampshade lined with a reflective foil. If we prefer to sacrifice light quantity for a softer, glowing effect, a translucent shade or an opaque bulb is more suitable. A pleated, fabric covered shade, as illustrated above, produces an even gentler effect. A shade can itself throw out patterned light; ridged glass or perforated shades can create a soft,

dappled ambient light. Care needs to be taken in the selection of such shades, however, as these effects can easily overpower a decorative scheme.

Scale is also very important when selecting a shade. Just as a piece of furniture should be of a size to complement a room, so a lamp should be in proportion to both. It is important that there should be a harmonious balance between the lamp base and the shade, and of the two with a decorative scheme – something that is, of course, particularly noticeable during the day.

You will find that to a greater or lesser degree most lamp bases are made from reflective materials to maximize rather than absorb the light. The table lamp on the right is made from antiqued brass, which has a period feel; others illustrated here are fashioned from either glass or perspex, suitable for almost any setting or colour scheme. While a coolie shade – even on a pendant, central light fitting – creates intimacy by throwing light and thus the room's focus towards the floor, the traditional Chinese paper globe lantern (illustrated overleaf) pro-

Lamp bases come in all shapes, sizes and materials and it is important to ensure that the choice of shade not only complements the style of a base, but is also in proportion with its size. Whether made of fabric, parchment, glass, metal or plastic, the pattern and colour of a shade must blend with the overall decorative scheme of the room.

duces warmth rather than intimacy, because it envelops the bulb, creating a glow, rather than a beam.

Providing good quality task light with minimal shadow is important for efficiency and to reduce eye strain. Good reading lamps need to have an appropriate wattage and be well positioned between eye and book. There is considerable value in using lamps with a movable armature, stable enough for the arm to be fully extended without the whole toppling over. Standard low-voltage halogen bulbs are excellent for task

ABOVE **Standard lamps are a fine choice for those winter evenings ensconced in your favourite** armchair. Modern adaptations include spots on flexible, adjustable stems that can be attached to the wall or to narrow stands.

LEFT **Directional light need not come only from spots in the ceiling. Anglepoise lamps with weighted** bases or lanterns suspended from thin wire can be placed to shine a light precisely over the required surface. They are functional and create interesting shapes or silhouettes against a wall or window.

use, particularly over food preparation surfaces in kitchens, because they give out a clear, cold light and a true colour rendition. However, unless they are used very carefully, either dimmed or to wash a warm coloured room scheme, their cool blue quality can easily chill a comfortable sitting room. Even in functional domestic spaces, ceilings that are heavily punctured with low voltage halogen downlighters to create a 'pepperpot' effect have an uncanny way of turning the space into something more akin to a public library.

The correct positioning of each light fitting, and the ease with which a design can be controlled, determine its success. Better a simple scheme on one circuit that is easy to use than one that promises every mood under the sun but is too fiddly or too complex to operate.

Having a number of different circuits is a great asset, allowing a number of fittings to be controlled at the same time so that the overall lighting scheme can accommodate different alternatives. Dimmer switches can then be used to balance these circuits to suit a particular time of day or occasion. Control systems that store a number of pre-set lighting 'moods' that can be established on

demand are now available. Switches can either be hidden or made into a feature, but their position should always take into account the paths we might take across a room and where we might need light to see our way safely to the next switch. The most convenient place for task-light switches tends to be in the immediate vicinity of the task itself.

Certain areas of a home bring into play their own particular problems. Lighting a conservatory can be tricky because it presents the challenge of a glass-covered space: artificial and natural light is lost into the garden or sky, rather than being reflected back into the room to provide a soft, ambient glow. In such cases, traditional rules of lighting design need to be modified. A conservatory is best lit with a number of low-intensity lights – they may be table, standard, wall bracket or low-voltage starlights – rather than a few bright ones. Sidelights are the most effective form of background lighting, whilst the high ceilings and sense of openness in a conservatory provide a natural setting for hanging lamps. It is also a good idea to incorporate exterior lamps, positioned in the garden or on the walls of the house, into the plan, to help bring a sense of the outside in.

KEYNOTES

- SELECTING LIGHT SOURCES

- BALANCING BULBS AND SHADES

- PENDANT AND TABLE LAMPS

- STYLES OF STANDING LAMP

- UPLIGHTERS AND DOWNLIGHTERS

- CANDLELIGHT, INSIDE AND OUT

- GENERAL, TASK, AMBIENT LIGHT

- PATTERNED AND COLOURED LIGHT

These highly individual table lamps, with their repeated geometric patterns and bold colours, act as a light sculpture in a contemporary room. The yellowish light cast by the square shades gives the room a mysterious atmosphere.

CANDLELIGHT

Despite the achievements of modern technology, simple candlelight remains the most attractive light of all. There is something special about light that is really alive and moving, and there is a primeval deference to fire. Candles provide lovely occasional lighting and their flickering warmth makes them a natural focal point. They may be conceived as simple candlesticks in the dining room or be floating with petals in water on a dining table; they may be thin beeswax tapers held in a bowl of sand on a sitting room floor or tiny nightlights in coloured glass holders in the bathroom.

In conservatories, candles may be placed in Moorish-style lanterns and suspended from the roof, or contained within the protective clear glass of hurricane lamps and hung on the walls. Outdoors, citronella candles that deter insects, or low-voltage waterproof lamps, can play with shade or shadow, providing intriguing night views for those inside to enjoy.

No other form of light creates quite the same mood as candlelight. It is soft and evocative, while the shadow play of pattern and texture around a room produces an ever-changing kaleidoscope.

A SUMMARY OF **THE ESSENTIALS**

The effect of design not only works on the senses but on our emotions too; the mood is our first consideration in designing a room.

ATMOSPHERE

DAYLIGHT

COLOUR

AMBIENT

DIRECTIONAL

SHADOW

REFLECTION

ABSORPTION

SPARKLE

ILLUSION

109

3

COLOUR

The permutations of three primary colours, their relationships and associations, seem to be the most challenging part of designing a room. Deciding on a colour scheme is the most tangible commitment to our idea of a particular room – its style, mood, uses and even perceived temperature. Colour has the capacity to effect the greatest transformation of a space, yet because it is so powerful many of us prefer to adhere to familiar neutrals rather than exploring its full potential. An understanding of how colours work in a design can encourage us to be more adventurous within our individual schemes.

LEFT A vase of fresh flowers is a simple and flexible way to brting vivid colour into a room.

PRINCIPLES OF COLOUR

An understanding of the relationships between colours is essential in decorative schemes

RIGHT The colours in this urban living room play with a palette of blue, pink and purple. The blues contain a hint of red to prevent them from appearing cold and to link them to the pinks and purples. Plain floorboards and creamy white paintwork provide a backdrop for the varied colours.

COLOUR PERCEPTIONS

Our reactions to colour are instinctive and often unquantified; consciously or not, we are constantly making judgements about the effect of colour in the world around us. Yet trying to choose colours for our own decorating schemes is often extremely hard. This is because a colour is not a constant, but changes according to light, climate, space and the other colours that we choose to put next to it. Understanding how colour works inside a house enables us to choose well from the wide range of options, and to make a successful imaginative leap from paint chart to living space.

Light is essential to the very existence of colour, and it shapes our responses to particular shades and tones. As light strikes an object, some is absorbed and some reflected; it is the reflected rays that determine the colour we perceive.

Even so, reactions to colours are not uniform – both eye and brain can be highly selective and subject to the tricks played by illusion and context.

DESIGNING WITH COLOUR

The hardest part of creating a colour scheme is knowing where to start. Because most of us lack confidence with colour, we tend to use safe, neutral shades which do not necessarily make

LEFT The large windows in this drawing room have played a part in the choice of its decorative colour. The walls are a light summer yellow, and curtains and sofa cushions are in co-ordinated fabrics. The deep red chair is carefully positioned so that its dark colour is offset by the shafts of sunlight.

the most of a space. Start by looking at the room in detail and pinpoint its characteristics. Is it small or large, bright or dark, and how does the light vary during the day? The amount of daylight a room receives, and whether that light is direct or indirect, will have an important impact on how colours appear. Consider how you plan to use the room, and the mood or range of moods you want to create. What you are after is a sense of balance. Even the mellowest scheme needs a vibrant note – however small – to bring it alive, while the most dramatic schemes need an element of quiet.

The natural relationship between paint colours is defined by the order in which they appear in the spectrum. This is based on the various relationships that each of the three primary colours – red, blue and yellow – have with each other, the way they blend or jar, like notes in an octave. The relationships between colours are often illustrated in a colour wheel or circle, as shown overleaf. The two key relationships involve opposing and adjacent colours within the circle. Their interaction lies at the heart of all colour scheming, and will determine its sucess in a particular setting.

BELOW Colour can have a strong impact on the atmosphere of a room and should be considered in choosing the decorative theme. These essentially restful turquoise walls are given a lively edge by the introduction of a decadent purple sofa. The upholstery's shiny texture reflects light back into the room.

ABOVE The sense of height in this converted mews house is exaggerated by the vertical yellow and white stripes on the walls of its galleried living area. The idea is echoed in the yellow of the cushions, white pillar and the strong vertical lines of the white balustrade.

RIGHT The skylight in this kitchen has brought a sense of uplift to an otherwise dark room with a low ceiling. The warm orange wall behind the Aga provides an intimate focal point and clearly defines the cooking and eating space.

LEFT Our sense of perspective can be influenced by the clever use of colour. The dark blue wall of this awkward staircase is spotlit by a skylight over the stairwell. Colour and lighting give the impression that the wall is some distance away.

BELOW Bright colours will emphasize a shape with confidence and flair. This exuberant swivel chair brings a strong focal point to an otherwise neutral room.

Complementary colours are those situated directly opposite each other in the circle: red/green, blue/orange and yellow/violet. These colours react strongly with one another. If they are placed side by side they become more vibrant and, in certain cases, they actually seem to flicker. Such effects have long been exploited by designers and artists for creative and commercial purposes. Oranges, for example, are often wrapped in purple tissue paper, and red meat is displayed against a grass green background. Analogous hues are those colours abutting one another in the colour circle, such as yellow, yellow-green and green. When used together, these close companions will complement one another visually. They work well because, to a greater or lesser extent, all share one dominant colour.

WARM AND COLD COLOURS

The division of colours into warm and cold hues provides a useful framework around which to construct an interior decorating scheme. Warm colours, such as reds and yellows, are dominant themes and make a room appear to 'approach', to close in upon you. They may make a space feel attractively intimate, or they may make it seem overwhelming or claustrophobic, depending on its size, aspect, shape and furnishings. In contrast, cool colours, such as blues and greens, appear to 'recede', to move out away from you. This creates a powerful illusion of space, especially if the palest versions of such colours are chosen. If used in small amounts as accents, cooler colours also bring a welcome relief to the effect of an overheated scheme.

Although red, yellow and orange are in their purest form warm colours, you will see by looking at the secondary ring on the colour wheel that they grow cooler the closer they venture towards their complementary colour. This creates cool, bluey reds, or greeny, acidic yellows; likewise, warm blues and greens are those that sit closer to red or yellow.

COLOUR RELATIONSHIPS

The colour wheel or circle is the basic tool used in the interpretation of colour. It illustrates the diversity of the colours of the spectrum in their correct sequence and reveals how they interact, or relate to, one another. It is a very useful guide for selecting colours and for practical colour mixing.

At the centre of the circle are the three primary colours of paint – red, yellow and blue – from which all other colours derive. Combining each primary colour with its neighbour produces the ring of secondary colours – orange, green and purple. The outer ring demonstrates the way

a secondary colour mixed with the adjacent primary colour produces a third generation of tertiary colours. The same pattern of

combining adjacent colours to produce different hues can continue until a full spectrum is created, with colours becoming more and more subtle.

Complementary colours are those diametrically opposed to each other in the circle: red/green, blue/orange and yellow/violet. These 'opposites' have a vibrancy when used together in decorative schemes. Analogous hues, which are the colours that sit next to each other in the colour circle – such as yellow, yellow-green and green – have a more harmonious relationship, for softer designs.

Despite its apparent coolness, blue and white is a very popular colour combination and is widely used throughout the home. The calm formality of this Swedish-style dining room, with its pale blue painted wooden floor and soft blue walls, is complemented by the femininity of the loose cotton chair covers and the gilt-framed mirror.

TINTS, SHADES AND TONES

Each colour within the colour circle is also the root of a vast family of tints, tones and shades, all of which retain the warmth or coolness of the original. These are known as the different 'values' of the colours and are very effective when used as highlights in a scheme. A tint is produced by the addition of white to a pure colour, reducing its strength and increasing its opacity; pink is actually a tint of red. A shade derives from the addition of black to a colour, which reduces its vividness and darkens it; maroon is thus a shade of red. A tone is created when grey is added to bring subtlety to a colour; it may sometimes be referred to as 'mid-tone'.

A colour may also be described in terms of its purity or strength. Its so-

Cushions are useful, versatile elements in a colour scheme. They may introduce bright accents or a neutral respite from other colours in a room. The creamy whites provide a visual space that enhances the stronger colours of the scheme.

KEYNOTES

• COMPLEMENTARY COLOURS

• COOLNESS AND WARMTH

• LIGHT AND SHADOW

• TEXTURE

• REFLECTION

• ABSORPTION

• BALANCING SHADES AND TONES

called 'intensity' can be measured as the degree to which it differs from grey. A colour in its purest state, unmixed and unmodified, is of the highest intensity. If grey or a complementary colour is added, it will reduce its intensity. For example, while pink is always red in hue, it ranges from a vivid, almost pure, pink (high intensity) to a more neutral, greyed pink with a softer impact (low intensity).

The intensity of a colour is not fixed; rather, it may appear to vary depending on the quality of the light striking it and adjacent colours. Context is thus critical: a red will seem to have a lower intensity if a red-orange (analogous) colour is placed next to it, and correspondingly a higher intensity if a green (complementary) colour is its neighbour.

One group of colours not included in the colour circle contains the neutrals based in black and white: greys, browns, beiges, creams, off-whites, and so on. They are an important feature in contemporary interiors, making rooms appear lighter, wider and taller whilst providing a useful complement to natural textures (see page 171). However, they need to be used carefully or they can make a room look bland.

CHANGING SPACES

Natural light changes dramatically with latitude, both in quantity and quality, and this in turn influences the resonance a colour will have in different parts of the world. In areas of steady, high quality, natural light, such as California, the Mediterranean and the Caribbean, the strong, mellow light suits clear pastels, strong hues and rich colours. The more mutable nature of the light in mid-northern Europe, however, means that a more muted decorating palette tends to be chosen. Because light intensity can fluctuate at different times of the year, care needs to be taken that the right colour tone is chosen for a room. What can seem to be a rich, full blue in summer can end up looking like the bottom of a pond by autumn.

Climate also exerts a subtle influence on the effect of colours in a room. Warm colours, for example, will work well in a north-facing room with a cold atmosphere. If a room has a warm, southerly aspect, you may wish to steer away from hot yellows and reds but opt for colours that will cool it down. Within this basic premise, there is scope for choice and creativity; these colours can be light, dark, rich or strong, depending on the size of the room. Lighter versions will enlarge the room and darker shades produce a more intimate feel.

The elegant, dining room with high ceilings illustrated opposite is lit by cool northern light during the day. Its cool blue and white scheme might seem too cold by itself, but the cream fabric of the

window treatment introduces a note of warmth. And the blue paint chosen for the walls, though pale, has a redness to it that removes the chill from the scheme.

Colour tones can vary across a room scheme to reflect each area's individual needs. The sitting room on page 118 uses a much cooler blue at the window, but is warmed by the flooring and the pink upholstery. In a larger area, a stronger version of these cool colours would not fight with the design.

The honey tones give unity and warmth to the large Tuscan room above by successfully tying in the vaulted ceiling – its dominant feature – and the earth colours of the landscape beyond.

The brightness of the light is a feature of the inside of the house as much as the outside. It reflects off the sawtooth patterning on the rich stair colours on the right to bring a feeling of width to a narrow area. Analogous colours (see page 117) have been used, so that even with the pattern a harmony is maintained.

COLOUR ACCENTS

While it is perfectly possible to use cold colours like blue and green in a north-facing room, keeping the warmth by using hues from the red/yellow ends of their spectrum, another useful way of balancing a predominantly warm or cold scheme is by using contrasting accents.

This could be a dash of repeated colour within a patterned or multi-coloured fabric, flooring or wall covering. If it also contains a tone of the room's pre-dominant colour, it will successfully harmonize with the various plain surfaces. These accents could also be relatively small, accessories such as cushions, picture mounts, or individual flower arrangements, which may change from season to season.

A strong focal point in a complementary colour can also deceive us into thinking that a room scheme is hotter or cooler than it really is. It can also mean that a red sofa in a cool blue room becomes even more seductive.

LEFT **The characteristic Tuscan colours of burnt umber, ochre yellow and rich sienna bring warm** earth tones to this vaulted living room. The furniture, soft furnishings and wall treatment create a relaxed and intimate mood.

ABOVE **Using shades of colour as pattern creates a novel design for a steep flight of steps, increasing** the sense of perspective and movement. The painting of the rises also has a practical intent, drawing attention to the irregular steps.

The striped cover of this simple wrought iron bed is echoed in the application of two faded colours in wider stripes on the walls. Blue and dull yellows are restful colours for a bedroom and imaginatively reinforce the natural theme.

Whilst they serve to establish a focal point in a room, distract the eye from an unattractive part or emphasize an asset, bold, contrasting colours are also useful to enliven small and narrow spaces and bring a vitality to otherwise neglected areas. These are the parts of a room that we generally try to 'lose' by playing them down with a more neutral palette, but using strong colour can be a much more exciting solution.

PIGMENTS AND DYES

The tangible aspect of colour in interior design is largely that of pigments and dyes. These vital ingredients have defined the colour of paints and inks, fabrics and fibres and glazes for ceramics for centuries. They determine not only the number of colours that are available to us, but also their depth and vitality, the degree to which they look different under various light sources, and the degree to which they change – in some cases disappear – with age.

Early dyes and pigments were all rock or vegetable extracts. Few were colour-fast and many succumbed to the deleterious effects of light. You need only look at early tapestries, for example, to see how the reds and blues have survived but that the less stable yellow and greens have almost completely disappeared. Pigments and dyes operate in a subtly different way. A pigment can be used as either a paint or dye; it coats and colours the surface but does not combine with it. A dye is a colouring matter that works as a stain, reacting chemically with the fibres and colouring them completely. A dye can achieve different results on different fibres, but a tanning substance or mordant must be present in the fabric for the chemical reaction to take place.

It is important to understand the difference between pigments and dyes when choosing colours for an interior. While we may wish for a perfect match of fabric and paint colour, the fundemental difference in the way each is coloured means that it will inevitably react to light in a different way. This fact remains even though over three million artificial and natural colouring substances are now available, and modern lighting developments have transformed the ways in which we can invent and reinterpret our homes.

REDEFINING
PERCEPTIONS OF COLOUR

Our responses to colour are never fixed; they can be influenced by shape, texture and lighting as well as other colours in the room

COLOUR SCHEMING

There are two basic types of colour scheme: harmonious and contrasting. The harmonious scheme is one that uses adjacent colours in the circle, and can be based on just two colours or more. Monochromatic schemes, in which one basic colour is used in a variety of different values and intensities, are also harmonious. Rooms decorated in this way need to combine a neutral hue, and work most successfully with the addition of contrasting accents and accessories.

Great care needs to be taken in selecting colours; tonal contrast is needed to prevent the scheme from becoming boring, yet all the colours need to be based on the same segment of the circle (see page 117). It is easy to produce abrasive 'clashes' in what seem to be harmonious combinations. For example, mixing turquoise, cornflower, Wedgwood and Prussian blue could be disastrous, as some are blue-green, some pure blue and some have a slightly pinkish cast.

Contrasting colour schemes are more stimulating than harmonious ones and can be created in several ways. A straightforward complementary scheme will use the two colours directly opposite one another in the circle. A range of dif-

ferent values, tints or tones of the colour can be used to create a decorative scheme of vivid contrast; for example, turquoise with terracotta or lilac with gold. These provide balanced mixtures of warm and cool colours. A contrasting scheme can nevertheless be used to create a serene atmosphere, as in the room on the right, where pistachio is teamed with a soft lilac. Opposite, the warm and cool blues of walls and furniture work in harmony, but vibrant, yellow-green apple acts as a complementary accent. Try putting your finger on the apple and view the colours without the green: even this relatively small area of colour makes an amazing difference to our perceptions. This manipulation of colour was a favourite technique of the Impressionists; Monet, for example, enhanced the bright greens of the fields at Argenteuil with the insertion of vivid red poppies.

COLOUR AND CONTEXT

It is virtually impossible to hold the memory of a single colour in our minds because we do not see colour in isolation, but always in the context of those around it. This explains why a colour scheme – the combination of several interacting colours within a space – is

ABOVE The simple clean line of the *chaise longue*, upholstered in pale green and outlined against the window, strikes a tranquil note against the pale lilac. Pastel tones provide accents as successfully as bold primary colours when shape and space are appropriate.

RIGHT Furniture can provide useful focal points of shape and colour. Contemporary ranges of furniture feature subtle shades, clear outlines and smooth textures which can reflect bright daylight back into a compact space.

more important to good design than the beauty of any single shade within it. If, for example, you look closely at the way colours in a painting interact, and the effect of light upon their relationship, you will soon see that we can learn a great deal about colour from an artist's selection and juxtaposition of particular shades, tints and tones. The combination of colours in a painting may provide a touchstone or concept for an actual scheme, or simply illustrate orthodox or innovative principles at work. It is interesting that celebrated painters such as Paul Klee and Wassily Kandinsky both taught colour theory to architects and interior designers at the German Bauhaus School of modernist design.

The interplay of colour and light, and how to illustrate it truthfully, was one of the defining principles of the Impressionist movement. Claude Monet's series of paintings of Rouen Cathedral, for example, reflects the fluctuating light effects through subtle changes in colour palette. He would work on one canvas at a particular point in the day and move to another an hour or so later as the light shifted in angle and quality. The Dutch artist Piet Mondrian, by contrast, employed strong bright colours and straight lines, balancing verticals and horizontals to achieve a geometric balance and purity. Mondrian's distinctive use of colour and shape inspired a range of designs, of interiors and accessories.

Such a transition between fine art and interior design is not entirely straightforward, however. Remember when considering colour on a canvas that light impacts differently upon a three-dimensional area than it does on a flat surface. Our perception of scale is also very different, and the relationship between the individual colours must not be assumed to be fixed.

DEFINING SPACE WITH COLOUR

The effect a colour has on a room will increase in proportion to the size of area on which it is applied. Whilst accents may bring a subtle correction or touch of luxury to the dominant scheme, the more it dominates and tips the balance,

RIGHT **Repetition of colour tones can reinforce and modify a particular scheme. The rust stripe of the** cotton floormat is echoed in the throw over one arm of the *chaise longue*, a pair of scattered cushions, the small painting on the wall and the edging of the linen blind, creating a coherent and imaginative look.

BELOW **Texture can affect the apparent colour of a fabric by changing the way in which light is reflected** or absorbed by its surface. A variety of textures brings definition and stimulus to a limited colour range, and even bland colours can assume a three-dimensional quality.

LEFT **Colours do not always have to contrast to work successfully. Tones and shades of the same base** colour, used for example in wall treatments and upholstery fabric, will highlight and continue a decorative theme. Some degree of contrast is helpful, however; this symphony of purple relies for effect on the neutrality of the beige with which it is combined.

the more impact it will have not only on other colours, but also on our awareness of shape, brightness and atmosphere.

Colour can also define our sense of perspective; although harmonious, the colour scheme applied in the two rooms leading from each other on the left serves to demarcate the two areas clearly. The nearer space has been painted in a pale purple that is nevertheless strongly represented. As we look through the doorway into the next room, the purple scheme is echoed in a deeper shade of the colour used for the upholstery, while the walls are left neutral. Both spaces work well together, but the proportions of colour in each room enable the nearer room to be more dominant without coming into conflict with the other room. It is also interesting to note how these colours tend to lean towards grey, but have been given a freshness by the complementary accent of a strongly contrasting green foliage and flower arrangement.

INTERPRETING COLOUR

Colours are not static: artificial and natural light can exert very different influences over the same area and produce different effects with a few hours. This makes colour matching in interiors particularly complex and is the reason why it should ideally be done after the installation of artificial lighting so that samples can be considered *in situ*. Even the colour of a lampshade can affect all the colours of a decorative scheme, and should always be tried over a working bulb before it is chosen – a point to bear in mind when choosing colours for

rooms that will be used mainly in the evening, a dining room, for example. Before reaching for a colour card, you need to consider the size of the space, the quality and quantity of the artificial light and the atmosphere that different colours are likely to dictate.

The first step towards putting together a successful colour scheme is to think about our own reactions to the colours that we see. These will be highly individual: some people have a natural preference for one colour that is quite the opposite for another person. Some, such as the abstract painter Kandinsky, even possess a highly sensual reaction to colour known as synaesthesia, whereby they experience colour sensations when other senses, such as taste and hearing, are stimulated. Although we all possess

Colour can transform our perception of an interior and the impact of accents and small features is often overlooked. Cushions, lampshades, even a skein of embroidery yarn will bring a different emphasis and texture to an overall scheme. Whether complementary or contrasting, they may redefine our response to larger areas of colour, such as curtains, carpets or upholstery.

RIGHT **The kitchen is a good place to experiment with an unorthodox combination of colours. Surfaces** and materials are boldly exposed, integral to the design of the room, without the additional considerations of furniture and fabrics.

LEFT **Texture and pattern can be used successfully to complement a monotone colour scheme. This** alternate matt and glossy stripe around a chimney breast creates an interesting decorative and visual effect without the need for a mirror or other accessory above the fireplace.

RIGHT Co-ordinated fabric is a favourite option to maintain the decorative continuity of a room. Curtains can echo the fabrics of cushions, loose covers for chairs or even wall treatments. It is also a way in which to introduce another colour to the overall scheme.

some shared preconceptions about colour – as children we were taught that the sky is blue and grass is green when experience tells us that this is often not the case – we may prefer one colour over another simply because we connect it with a particular memory, attitude or observation. Some people have a natural colour coherence in the decoration of their homes because one preferred colour or combination unwittingly predominates in the scheme. Our reaction to one particular colour can also depend on the colours that are placed adjacent to it; a cool colour positioned against one set of colours may read as a warm one when viewed against a different set.

One useful way of creating a colour scheme is to draw inspiration from an existing feature of the room, such as the floor or wall covering, a patterned fabric or even a favourite painting or accessory that incorporates several colours. Even if the chosen colour plays only a minor part in the pattern from which it derives, the combination should still work when the balance is shifted. A skilfully chosen painting, for example, may provide an integrating focal point for different colours in an overall scheme that is designed around it.

COLOUR AND TEXTURE

One of the most effective techniques that designers possess is the use of different textures to create a subtle demarcation between very similar colour tones. This introduces an interesting pattern that does not have too strong an effect. The room opposite, for example, has been decorated with horizontal stripes of a very similar tone. Contrast lies in its reflective quality; as the matt

stripe signals its colour constantly, the reflective stripe only reveals colour from certain angles. The room's high ceilings appear wider under the influence of these horizontal lines (see page 30), yet a harmonious balance is maintained by the strong vertical accents of fireplace surround, lamp stands and radiator bars. Any tension in the textured pattern is reduced by the use of a dado rail, the area below which is decorated with plain

Sometimes a textile is of such a striking colour that it dominates an entire space. This unusual bed with a curved iron frame has drapes of deep golden yellow tied artistically around it; another piece swirls about the lampshade. The exotic, multi-coloured bedcover accentuates both the yellow and the tranquil pale green of the walls.

white paint. The simple cubic lamp-shades on the mantel shelf bring a further twist to the linear theme, prompting us to wonder how the room would look in artificial light.

COLOUR TO MAXIMIZE LIGHT

The judicious use of strong colour can bring a great deal of power to a decorative scheme, yet, especially if space is limited, we still regard neutrals or pastels as the safer option. The reason for our preference is that they are the colours that will reflect the most light, a quality that we see as an overriding attribute. This is in stark contrast to preferences for vibrant colours in the 19th and early 20th centuries, where less efficient heating, cleaning and insulation meant that an illusion of cosiness was highly valued.

These days we take background warmth, if required, for granted and we prefer to stress the modern luxury of space. Our first response to this desire is usually to reach for a pot of white paint. White will bounce available light into every nook and cranny and thus enhance a feeling of space – more so if it has a reflective finish – and when used in a room with other colours will be given interest as it picks up reflected colour. Matt white is,

above all, the king of contemporary ceilings. It reflects more light than any other colour and promotes height. This point should be borne in mind if a room has a disproportionately high ceiling, as even the most subtle wash of colour may be enough to lower it and improve both its sense of proportion and atmosphere.

You only need look at the number of different white paints that are available today to see just how dominant its use has become in decoration. 'Natural whites', which include a minute tint of another colour, are another variation of this key trend, although care needs to be taken in their use as they often prove more strongly coloured than expected.

The use of three or four shades of off-white to paint the different planes of woodwork – be they doors, architraves or skirting – has long been used by designers as a means of accentuating their relief and giving a room space and depth. When they are combined in such a way that the tones run from dark at the base to light as they reach the cornice, they can be used successfully to 'lift' the visual impact of a whole room.

Although you may feel that it gives light and space to a room, it would be wrong to consider white an easy option.

KEYNOTES

• HARMONY AND CONTRAST

• PROPORTION

• SIZE AND SHAPE

• INTENSITY AND VALUE

• PERSPECTIVE

• ACCENTS

• COLOUR RELATIONSHIPS

The tongue and groove walls of this kitchen have been painted in bright red gloss, the simple table covered in a thin layer of copper and the floor also painted with gloss, so that the entire room reflects any available light from the small window.

So-called 'pure' whites can be impossible to match (as becomes clear when you are buying white ceramic baths and basins and find so much colour variation between ranges). White can be demanding to accommodate, and may appear too functional in a mono-chromatic scheme. It is possible to enliven such schemes with different textures; combining translucent marble, white damask and the weave of canvas or linen, for example, will add depth and stimulus to an essentially plain scheme.

COLOUR AND REFLECTION

Perceptions of colour are known to be determined by light reflecting off an object's surface; it follows, therefore, that reflection is an important factor in any design scheme.

As a rule, matt surfaces reflect little surface light and allow colour to be read easily. A gloss or polished surface, on the other hand, will reflect shine as well as colour. This can give vibrancy and energy to the colour, because as the eye moves so the reflection dances and the colour is visually interrupted and continually reassessed. Highly reflective surfaces such as glass coffee tables and metal handles produce bright, dominant accents in a room; this may be especially useful where natural light levels are low.

Matt surfaces, by contrast, are useful in a very light space where competing reflections from several surfaces may cause uncomfortable glare. Reflections increase the impact of colour in a space and by bringing more light into a room can make it appear physically larger.

The effect of colours in a room is thus not always predetermined. Red, known as an 'advancing' colour that reduces the sense of space, can have a very different effect if a high degree of reflection is used along with it and good light is supplied. In the imaginative scheme illustrated above, even the ceiling has been treated in red, yet because light is encouraged to reflect from all surfaces, including the floor, the feeling of space is maintained. This stimulating use of colour and surface can work particularly well in social areas, such as dining rooms, which benefit from the use of warm and inviting colours. By going even further and illuminating the space with candles, the flicker and vitality will enhance the reflective effect while the room retains its colour warmth.

MOODS OF COLOUR

Choosing colours involves the design and size of the space, as well as the atmosphere we want to create

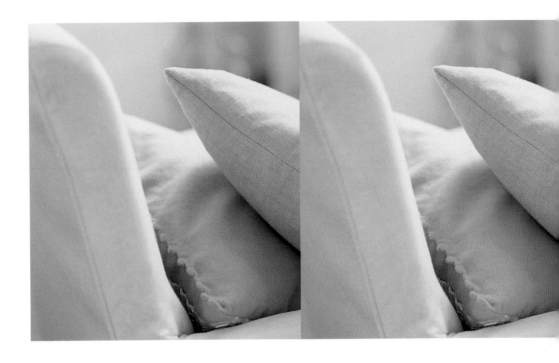

Natural upholstery fabrics bring a calm, contemporary feeling to a room. This may be enhanced by textural features such as self-covered buttons or the trimming or piping on a chair seat. Contrasting colour tones highlight the decorative features and shape our responses to the overall design.

ASSOCIATIONS OF COLOUR

Our reactions to colour are never entirely neutral. Whether or not we are aware of it, we bring with them a variety of associations and expectations that decorative schemes can either reinforce or challenge. We sense instinctively that certain objects – be they functional or decorative – work better in some colours than others. The same is true of spaces: the contemporary chic of a streamlined kitchen will require an entirely different colour palette to a romantic period bathroom. Cultural and historical resonances will also shape our interpretation of colour; white, for example, is a symbol of death and mourning in the East and is therefore seldom chosen for interiors. We may choose to confront traditional connotations of colour, but

they should not be ignored; it is wise to explore them in detail when planning an interior scheme.

Colour has a powerful effect upon the emotions, and has long been recognized as having a direct influence on how people feel in a room. The way in which individual shades are combined is all-important. Adjacent, harmonious hues from the colour circle (see page 117) are generally relaxing and easy to live with, and either warm or cool colours can provide the basis for such a scheme, depending on the particular space. A cool, fairly pale, monochromatic arrangement that creates an illusion of greater space and light can be broken up with forms, shapes and textures that react differently to sources of light. If the scheme is based on just two colours,

133

LEFT Flowers provide a flexible and decorative keynote for a room and offer the chance to experiment with flashes of bright, localised colour. Not only the colour tones but also the associations of the flower are important influences on the space; peonies convey a sense of luxurious, refined beauty.

in a decorative scheme. They harmonize naturally and can introduce a sense of serenity to an interior. Nature's colour palette ranges right across the spectrum, from greys, browns and terracotta earth tones to the blues and greens of water, sky and vegetation.

HEAT AND DUST

Warm decorating colours include a wide variety of the available reds, oranges and yellows; they are stimulating and dominant, with a tendency to 'advance' into the room. Pure red has a boldness that may be overpowering if used to excess and it often works most successfully as a dramatic accent colour. Pale tints of red (pinks) and greyed versions (dusty rose and plum) are more subtle, warm colours that work well in cold rooms. Burgundy and plum tones create a feeling of warmth and quiet elegance, bringing a relaxing air of luxury to traditional living and dining rooms. Orange is an intense colour of vitality and energy, and like red works best as an accent colour in relatively dark rooms. In its purest hue, it is too dominant to be used over a large area, but when lightened it becomes the more delicate, welcoming colour of peach or apricot. The peach

remember that they do not have to be used equally throughout the space, or they will appear overly regimented. A better option is for one colour to dominate and the other to supplement, either by using it to highlight details or to work as a feature within a particular area.

A complementary colour scheme uses direct opposites from the colour circle, balancing coolness and warmth and creating contrast and interest. Rooms decorated in this way tend to feel lively

and active, although they can be toned down to achieve a calm, more harmonious atmosphere. The balance of one colour against another, either through intensity or area, is crucial to the final result. Unlike an harmonious scheme, which is already balanced, a complementary design leans towards the dominance of one of the two colours, which may need careful adjustment.

It is interesting to see the effect that colours from the natural world can have

coloured peonies shown opposite provide a delightful accent against the complementary green of the vase. When greyed down, orange becomes terracotta or a soft brick colour, popular – like a yellow/brown ochre – as a colour wash in cooler climates because of its association with the sun's heat and energy.

Yellow, the brightest portion of the colour spectrum, is a joyful and stimulating colour that has resonances of sunshine and gold. In the contemporary

kitchen above, the intense combination of yellow and black is modified into a more sophisticated citron and slate grey, colours with natural associations that are pertinent to an area designed for the preparation of food.

Bright yellows are advancing colours that reflect a lot of light and can therefore be used on fairly large surface areas, even in small spaces. They bring warmth to dull, sunless rooms and are also a useful complement to the natural light

ABOVE **The introduction of radical new colour into a design can produce a new dimension of pattern** and a strong focal point. The monotone colour scheme of this kitchen is enlivened by contrasting citron yellow units, which also increase the physical impact of the black table.

LEFT **A complex tonal colour palette has been used in this living room to evoke an exotic, sophisticated** feel. The palest of yellows and murky mauves of upholstery and bolsters highlight the interesting variety of shapes and textures. The colours contrast very subtly with the uneven turquoise colourwash on one wall.

received in a bright room. Pale yellow can also make small, dark rooms appear larger and brighter, while greyed yellows, in the form of subtle mustards, golds and golden-browns, can create warm colour schemes that echo the earth tones of the natural world.

Blue tones, associated with the sea and sky, encompass many colours, from light grey to turquoise. Blue is a cool, receding colour that can provide a room with a feeling of calm and tranquillity, as well as airiness and space. Pale shades in particular create a refreshing, restful environment acknowledged to lower blood pressure and relieve insomnia, making it the perfect choice for a bedroom or sitting room. Blue is frequently used in combination with white, but it also harmonizes well with warm colours, such as yellow – dark blue and gold, or sky blue with citrus, are classic combinations in art and design. Sometimes felt to be rather cold when used to excess, blue is given depth and warmth by complements of cream and red. The liveliness of turquoise or peacock blue are valuable as bright accents, particularly in dark areas, as they reflect a lot of light. Blue purples take on a warm hue that creates harmonious yet exciting rooms.

Violet and purple are rich, vibrant and regal colours, which in their strongest values can be overpowering and hard to use. However, they can become good accents if used in combination with neutral or pastel contrasts. Pastel versions – lilac and mauve – will be either cold or warm, depending on the amount of blue or red in the colour; both can be used effectively to create romantic, feminine rooms. The deeper, greyed, plum tones

Sometimes a strong sense of colour can impose coherence upon the most daring combination. The bold stripes of this sofa are surprisingly not at odds with the multi-coloured border of the carpet. Its red, blue and yellow hues are then reinforced by cushions, armchair and displayed artwork.

LEFT Colour can highlight or camouflage individual pieces of furniture. The vibrant shade of this lime-green sofa emphasizes its individual shape; background colours are kept relatively neutral to allow the furniture to dictate the pace.

RIGHT Colour can change mood in even small areas of a room. This quiet corner for reading and relaxing works well thanks to a mix of warm and subdued terracottas.

BELOW RIGHT Stripes are visually exciting, bringing movement and perspective to a room. Here, the broad stripe livens up jaded chairs in a cool yet vibrant pattern. The yellow stripe is more acidic in tone than that of the wall — a daring play of colour.

are complex colours that are not easy to use, but they bring a rich, warm and mysterious note to a scheme.

Green is one of the most flexible decorating options, possessing a remarkable variety of colours, values and intensity. It is the colour most strongly associated with nature and is therefore experienced as regenerative and restful. This special quality is explained by the fact that green is strategically poised half way between the warm and cool colours of the circle. Shades range from acidic lime and fresh apple to complex olive and the subtle blue-green of pine, and as a receding colour creates an impression of expansion and space.

Strong yellow-greens, such as lime, provide vibrant, stimulating colours best used as accents in a neutral or rich, warm scheme. The richer greens of vegetation can help to 'bring the garden inside', especially if a scheme is complemented by the natural greenery of indoor plants. A dark room can be transformed by introducing the vivid delicacy of lighter green ferns and fronds. The addition of blue to green creates elegant, ice-cool tones; and if red and orange are mixed in, the warm brown-greens of the forest are made.

Our homes are both private space and public face; a clean

canvas upon which to project ideas about ourselves

Items of furniture that blend with a room's predominant colour scheme are a clever way to draw attention to tones. This sophisticated room develops pale on pale green in layers, bringing the shades into sharp focus with a contrasting purple cushion.

NEUTRAL AND NATURAL COLOURS

The true neturals are black, grey and white, none of which appear in the colour wheel. However, the term is often extended to included the so-called 'naturals' – browns, beiges, creams and off-whites – that have dominated the domestic landscape in recent years. Whilst some have been used in inappropriate spaces without sufficient thought, they do work well if properly balanced, especially if textural contrasts, such as wicker, wood and rattan, are introduced.

Natural colours tend to be used in a scheme to provide a link or a contrast, although in fact an entire room can be orchestrated around them. They can produce a cool, receding effect and evoke a sense of calmness and subtle stability by their association with the external natural world. Natural colours such as cream, sand and stone are enlivened with touches of strong, bright colours, although they often work well on their own. If colours are to be introduced into a neutral scheme, those with earth associations, such as brick, Indian reds and indigo blue, complement their inherent softness. However, because these so-called neutrals do still contain elements of their original, stronger hues, any colour chosen to accent them has to be considered very carefully.

Black and grey are sombre colours that need the relief of other hues. Black hardly exists in nature – even the darkest material will normally be a very dark variation of another colour. Neutral grey occurs when all light rays of the spectrum falling on an object are absorbed to the same degree. Grey may be mixed from black and white, or from any pair of complementary colours.

Used in small quantities, black can sharpen any colour scheme, but unless it is introduced with considerable care it can dazzle or appear uncomfortable. Pure pale grey will tend to take on some of the colour with which it is used, and can therefore appear either warm or cold accordingly. Greys provide a useful note of contrast in dark or very warm decorative schemes.

In the West, a colour of purity and innocence, white is the natural background against which all other colours play their part. It is an essential neutral and should be used with specific intent rather than to play safe. It has many virtues – it is cool and calming; it can freshen up other colours; it harmonizes well with primary colours; and it gives a dramatic, classic look if used with black.

HISTORICAL COLOURS

Historically, the colour we have introduced into our homes has been entirely dependent on what has been available. To begin with our palette was based almost exclusively on locally available earth colours and vegetable dyestuffs: soft drabs, yellows, reds, sienna browns and, later, indigo. All are naturally mellow hues, a characteristic that still keeps them desirable keynotes in any 'historic' paint chart. While foreign travel and trading over the centuries have encouraged the introduction of new colours, it is in their combinations that the tastes of

a particular period are revealed. Light, fanciful pairings, such as rose Pompadour with Sèvres blue, typify the French rococo; strong lilacs, black and silver typify the Art Deco period; and travellers on the 18th-century Grand Tour returned wanting to recreate the Etruscan schemes of red and black.

Though a muted palette has always suited our light, pure intense colour has always been highly prized. When a commercial source of a desired colour was discovered – such as the ground lapis lazuli that produced an intense ultramarine – it was invariably expensive and is one reason why we imbue rich blues, purples and greens with a sense of opulence. Only when chemists discovered synthetic aniline dyes in the 19th century, prompting the most lurid schemes, such as citric yellow and magenta, was almost any colour suddenly available.

KEYNOTES

- NATURAL INSPIRATIONS
- FABRICS AND TEXTURE
- BALANCE
- CLASSIC COMBINATIONS
- PATTERN AND PROPORTION
- REFLECTION
- ABSORPTION
- AUTHENTICITY
- RECEDING, ADVANCING COLOURS

ABOVE **Yellow and red is not an easy interior colour combination to adapt, and it relies on a careful choice** of similar tones and of quantities of each colour. Earthy red is used here in perfect proportion to ochre yellow.

LEFT **These elegant cushions combine different shapes, colours and textures in their visual impact. The wide stripes** reflect light in varying degrees and provide a complementary background to the central geometric panels. Crisp piping in contrasting texture and colour tones defines each cushion's shape.

The colour that completely skewed our palette was brilliant white. A colour that first arrived as a derivative of titanium oxide after the First World War, its cool clarity bears little relationship to any other colour that we see around us. Now, with the increased use of plastics and optical brighteners to produce fluorescent and pearlized paint finishes, there has been something of a backlash, a desire to return to more 'natural' colours and those that work well with the period of our homes.

In many cases, this fashion for imitating the original is unrealistic. The use of original vegetable dyes to colour any great quantities of fabrics is uneconomic, and the lead oxide that once gave paint its soft density would be foolhardy to reintroduce today. However, as a number of companies have recently, and successfully, discovered, the gentle mutability achieved with paints that have more pigment and less plastic, together with fabrics whose subtle colouration ages naturally, has enormous appeal. These are types of colour that have, if you like, a sense of humanity about them that puts us back in touch with our natural surroundings.

ABOVE LEFT **Contrast of colour and texture is interesting and stimulating. The density of this dark,** capacious sofa is rescued from gloom by the pale stripe of a pair of cushions. The texture of both sofa upholstery and cushion fabric is defined by daylight entering through a side window.

ABOVE **Placing white against black creates a stark, classic antithesis which works well in very diverse** materials. A softer effect, illustrated on the towelling fabrics, can be achieved by the subtle blending of similar shades. A stripe of white or strong complementary colour introduces contrast without discord.

MANIPULATING
COLOUR

Balancing colour and light allows us to develop our own interpretations of space and materials

COLOUR AND ILLUSION

So far we have considered the impact of colour as a solid, unchanging surface treatment, like paint on a wall. However, its role in decorating schemes is actually much greater than this, as it can be used to manipulate the spaces in which we live. Colour offers the potential to conceal and distract, create tricks and illusion and blur the boundaries between inside and outside space. As with light and shape, the secret is to use the special effects of colour judiciously; too many may result in a shallow space like a stage set that has lost any feeling of integrity and depth.

AGEING AND TEXTURE

Because a change in colour is a means by which we can judge the age of a surface – metal flecked with bright orange indicates the presence of rust, for example, while the grey/green on a stone ornament shows lichen and a natural weathering – so we can cheat age with colour too. Creating the illusion of age, either on pieces of furniture or areas of a room, can increase a sense of longevity or can harmonize with genuine age. The wall illustrated above, for example, has employed a technique whereby one

colour is rubbed on to another to give an ancient, ethnic, hand-produced feel. This theme is carried further by the choice of textile and spear-like curtain pole. It is a strong, exciting combination, thrown into relief by the cool adjacent wall and ceiling.

The intriguing combination of old with new has become an important interior style in itself, and can be accommodated in very different living spaces. It works effectively on a relatively small scale, as contrasts in the apparent age of objects can bring a new interest and focus to a

ABOVE **A wall treatment is often a scene setter, a thematic background for a striking fabric,** clever pattern or intriguing design. The use of non-matt colourwash on a bathroom wall complements the irregularity of the hand-painted curtain fabric.

BELOW **Ornaments can be used to bring emphasis or contrast to a colour scheme. Glassware is well** suited for either task. It can introduce additional colours and is constantly influenced by subtle changes of light.

tones of its furniture, is in fact very contemporary and yet it evokes associations with a slightly bohemian style of furnishing popular after the first World War. A feeling of authenticity, of having arrived at some valuable point of reference, is an important keynote in many modern homes. In the kitchen opposite, designed by the architect Frank Lloyd Wright, this feeling is reflected in the integrity of the wooden surfaces and in the room's tobacco-like colour scheme. In an inversion of a common modern decorating trick, the dark ceiling, used in a paler tone on the wall, makes the room appear lower and more compact – a simple, sustaining and protective base in which the character of the wood, and its association with permanence and stability, can be allowed to dominate.

THE ART OF ILLUSION

Colour and light can combine to alter or even create an illusion of space. The most dramatic way of doing this is with *trompe l'oeil*, which provides a sense of depth and perspective where none actually exists. Fine artists have used this technique for centuries to enhance individual spaces, ranging from the subtle suggestion of a recessed panel to the

room. Artefacts and antiques can be highlighted by displaying them against a backdrop of sleek modern materials. A featured brick or stone surface can be contrasted with smooth new walls to throw its texture into relief. In the larger picture on the previous page, the clever placement of different elements has established both a harmonious colour scheme and a contrast, although similar materials have been used. The perfect surface of a modern glass shelf and its brackets highlights the imperfections of the handmade glass bowls that are displayed on it. Colours and materials may be harmonious, but the pieces contrast.

DEFINING THE THEME

Colour is an essential element in shaping the particular style of a space. Historically authentic paints are one way of re-engaging with a room's past and celebrating its permanence and domestic roots. Yet this is not the only means of creating an atmosphere; the lightness of most modern interiors, that now have stronger and safer glass and more reliable power supplies, results in the corresponding projection of a period feeling into rooms by the use of darker furnishings and deep, rich colourings. The sombre decoration of the panelled sitting room above, offset by the warm

LEFT **A sitting room on the top floor of a former watchtower is naturally lacking in large windows, so the** ceiling has become the decorative focus. It has been painted in *trompe l'oeil* as if the octagonal coffers have fallen into disrepair and the ceiling is about to come down.

more fanciiful view of a fictional landscape through a window. In the vaulted room opposite, the ceiling has been painted to suggest domed and decorative octagonal coffers. While on the one hand the painted ceiling serves to reduce the small, ugly window to an insignificant feature, the natural daylight still highlights the ceiling's true structure, thus complementing the artist's work. Two important points contribute to the overall success of using *trompe l'oeil*. The first is the position of the viewer; if this can be somehow limited, in accordance with fixed lines of perspective, the effect is more credible. Secondly, the lighting of the coloured surface and the direction in which it is lit are significant. Much of the sensation of depth is conveyed by casting shadows in paint; if these do not correspond to the actual light used in a space, conflicting information is given to the viewer and the illusion fails.

Deceiving the eye by painting one material to imitate the appearance of another, more desirable material has been the art of the specialist wood grainer or marbler for hundreds of years. It relies upon the skilful layering and feathering of paint and transparent glazes to achieve the depth of marble or polished wood. The success of the technique depends on an understanding not only of the colouration of a particular material, but also of the way it would originally have been installed. If well executed, the result can be quite dramatic. The small bathroom illustrated above relies entirely upon paint effect for the textured impression given by its walls.

The application of colour to a surface is a useful way to conceal and distract from weak or ugly areas of a room, and it can also provide a focal point. Although many period rooms have used this technique to their advantage, it also works in modern spaces to bring an element of humour or surprise into the scene. Be aware, however, that the increased volume of natural light in our homes now makes it more difficult to fool the eye in this way.

Sometimes the proportions of a room need to be very subtly tinkered with to bring them into line. A room's width can be narrowed with a slightly darker tone on one wall of the colour of the other two walls; or it can be increased by using a slightly lighter tone on one of the walls. As we have seen, the properties of cool and warm colours can also contribute to

KEYNOTES

- CONCEALING

- HIGHLIGHTING

- PERSPECTIVE

- CONTINUITY AND DEMARCATION

- SIZE AND SHAPE

- ANTIQUING AND AGEING

- ILLUSION AND *TROMPE L'OEIL*

LEFT The introduction of a lighter band of colour between wall and ceiling is an established technique for raising the ceiling height. A practical and decorative wall cabinet picks up the lighter colour to give definition and depth to the storage cubes.

our perception of a space and increase either its sense of expansion or intimacy. This equation can be quite complex when using colour to demarcate different areas within a larger space, and when playing with the individual properties and character of each. In the living room on the left, a clever combination of primary colours creates three separate rooms, which work individually or together to evoke a lighthearted, up-beat atmosphere. Although white is used on the woodwork, the curtains and in the stripe on the balcony to unify the scheme, each space has been allowed to develop an atmosphere of its own. Each room within the space has developed an individual character, but not one that is so overpowering that it becomes physically separated from the next.

Strong primary colours have been employed to decorate the two levels of this cleverly designed room. Clearly defined colour schemes emphasize the demarcation of various spaces, whilst accents of yellow and red retain visual coherence across the space as a whole.

A SUMMARY OF **THE ESSENTIALS**

Like each note in the octave, every colour has its own character and relationships, based on its place in the spectrum.

ASSOCIATION

CONTRAST

HARMONY

LIGHT

TONES

INTENSITY

ACCENTS

ADVANCING

RECEDING

ATMOSPHERE

4

MATERIALS AND TEXTURE

The materials with which we clad or furnish a room will, like colours, contribute to its mood. Apart from functionality, our choice will lie in texture. Hard, shiny chrome or glass triggers a completely different response to soft fabrics or the organics like wood and wicker that lie comfortably between the two. Whether we choose a sleek modern look or the homespun associations of natural materials, an understanding of the building's structure will help to ensure an harmonious scheme. A successful design will harness both a material's intrinsic qualities and its finish to create contrast and balance.

LEFT Rich curtain fabric and carved wooden bedpost evoke a sense of stability and longevity in a traditionally styled space.

UNDERSTANDING
MATERIALS AND
TEXTURE

Materials shape the structure and fabric of a building and bring their individual characteristics to interior design

RIGHT **The Art Deco entrance hall to Claridge's Hotel in London has been designed using an interesting** combination of reflective materials. A tall mirror, polished dark woods, silver leaf columns and contrasting black and pale marble floor create a bright, sophisticated atmosphere.

CHOOSING MATERIALS

You only have to look around the room you are in to realize the extent to which materials shape and define our living space. Their textures and surfaces influence the play of light and effect of colour, and they refine and modify the atmosphere in a room. Such an exercise also makes us very aware of the physical structures that sustain a building – its walls, ceilings, floors, stairs – and its relationship with the outside world.

The wide range of building and surfacing materials now available presents us with complex choices, and it is necessary to understand the properties and impact of a particular substance fully before it is included in a design. Modern technology has brought materials once considered 'industrial', such as aluminium, perspex, fibreglass and even high-tension cable, into a domestic environment. These can feature as accents or be adopted wholesale to produce a sophisticated, contemporary look that relishes its own artifice. More traditional, natural textures are also now available in stronger, more durable forms than before. These enable us to create a simpler, rustic style, drawing upon materials from all over the world.

From cast iron to wool, the materials that we can use all possess their own characteristics, potential and limitations. Whether the immediate concern is for flooring or window treatments, wall coverings or furniture, the essential design questions will be the same. We need to bear in mind both practical requirements and the aesthetic needs of a room; the style and texture of materials used in its construction, as well as the decorative elements and cladding that are added later, will combine to shape a room's atmosphere. It is only too easy to overlook the messages and opportunities that are offered by the building itself, and so run the risk of working against integral materials and textures instead of in harmony with them. This can create an incoherent design and, ultimately, an unsettling environment.

When you are trying to work out which furniture, materials and finishes to choose, try to remember what it was that influenced you when you came to select your home in the first place. It helps to recognize that you have already taken the first steps in making a choice because something about the space attracted you. The style and period of the building may have influenced you, or possibly the

The mirrored doors of this cupboard have been painted with a delicate scene of birds and flowers. The painted design softens the reflected image and gives the doors an attractive, three-dimensional effect.

RIGHT The distressed paintwork of
this rustic dresser focuses attention on the real wood behind the
painted facade. Such stripping
away of ornament to reveal the
authentic material behind has
changed our perceptions of dilapi-
dation in a decorative scheme.

LEFT AND BELOW Combining different
materials gives additional depth
and impact to details within a
room. The peeling bleached frame of
a rustic mirror complements antique
glass from which the silvering is
wearing away. A smaller textural
accent is provided by a wooden bowl
of smooth round pebbles, in which
matt and reflective surfaces are
held in balance.

area or position. These influences should
not govern a design scheme, but rather
provide a framework within which to
operate. A building's location and architecture will to some extent limit what is
feasible: no amount of glazed chintz will
change a loft space into a country house,
nor will quantities of chrome and glass
transform a beamed cottage into an airy
flat. Nevertheless, a careful choice of
materials will do a great deal to improve
any individual space.

The characteristics of favoured materials need to be considered against the
strengths and shortfalls of the location in
which they will be used. Whether they
are soft, hard, ribbed, opaque or transparent, all materials have a natural
texture that will affect our reaction to a
room. How each material interacts with
others in the vicinity will determine its

role: to produce a contrast, reduce the
starkness of too much reflection or
become a feature in its own right. Specific textures will vary between types of
the same substance – for example, the
colours and grains of woods and the
structure of different granites. Although
certain attributes lie deep within the
basic substance, others depend on how
the material is finished. Glass, for
instance, can be rendered clear, tinted,
patterned or opaque. The flexibility finishes allow is a huge bonus, as materials
can be modified for a particular scheme.

It is important to think laterally about
the choice of materials to help solve a
room's problems. If the area is dark and
relatively small, introducing more light
will maximize the feeling of space. This
may be done through reflections from
mirrors, either direct or indirect. The

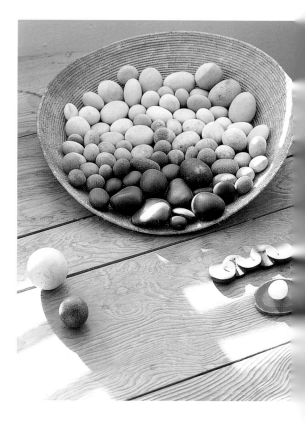

The warmth and colour of richly textured fabrics enhances the effect of smooth plastered walls and rough floor matting. Wall hangings, tapestries, cushions and rugs blend harmoniously into the historical theme.

painted mirror doors pictured on page 154, for example, show fauna and flora that complement the bedroom design and partially screen the view of the bed. It avoids the harshness of accurate reflection, providing the room with added depth and light in a softer, more sympathetic way than a completely smooth mirror.

Nor is glass the only reflective medium able to bring more light into a room. Hard and shiny surfaces, including metals, gilding and lacquerwork, even heavily polished furniture, dramatically increase the levels of general light. They influence our responses to colour (see page 112) and to the materials themselves. Pale, polished floors are highly reflective, though care must be taken to ensure they do not introduce too cold an atmosphere to the room. The gleaming dark woods of Art Deco-style pilasters, complemented by sparkling silver leaf, bring a cool, reflected light and spaciousness into Claridge's Hotel in London, illustrated on page 155. The shape of the mirror here is accentuated by vertical and horizontal lines that break up the image like a window pane to bring a feeling of both width and movement to the elaborate hallway.

MATERIALS AND FINISHES

Materials that form the structure of a building can often provide a key to the successful design of its interior. Their characteristics may be changed through finishing if required – stone, for example, is always cold and heavy, but its surface may be roughly textured or highly polished like marble to reflect more light. Materials can set the tone of a space; highly polished surfaces will produce a very different mood to that created by informal, warm, matt finishes.

The ability to re-finish a material is not a once-only operation but something that can recur throughout its life. Wood is one of the most attractive and versatile materials for finishes, which can radically alter its impact in a room. The diverse types of wood conjure up very different associations – from comfort-able, domestic pine and more solemn, weighty oak to the lighter, exuberant tones of beech and maple, the choice of many bright modern homes. With regular polishing, wood can take on a silky smooth lustre, which particularly enlivens dark coloured hardwoods such as mahogany and teak. However, less formal, unfinished wooden surfaces have their own story to tell. For example, a stripped pine mirror may have begun life as a gilded frame; its rough texture may still show evidence of the fine white plaster that once provided a perfect base for the gold leaf.

As paint or polish is worn away by use it creates a patina, or colouring, of age, investing the material with a comfortable, hospitable look. This antique impression can be successfully simulated using many different techniques to bring

RIGHT **The complex crossroads in this period house brings several materials into the design. A stone-**flagged floor contrasts with wooden stairs and woven wool rugs, while plaster reliefs introduce a three-dimensional quality to painted walls. The smooth marble column provides a valuable focus and anchor for this region of movement and transition.

BELOW **A sense of perspective can be exaggerated by using different materials and textures between** adjacent rooms. Paint effects and special wall treatments can appear to alter the size and shape, and different flooring materials will clearly demarcate each space.

PROPERTIES OF MATERIALS

Wood remains one of the world's most widely used building materials. The various colours, textures, cuts, treatments and finishes offer immense flexibility. A living material, wood can be destroyed by its innate dampness, whilst its knots, splits and grain make it individual, inconsistent and yet immensely powerful. Wood is not only strong in tension *along* the grain but also strong in compression *across* it. These fundamental properties have resulted in special techniques of construction that have shaped architecture and interiors for centuries.

The term 'masonry' encompasses bricks and tiles, as well as concrete and stone. These materials are strong in compression and weak in tension, and it is the weight of a brick or slab of stone that is relied upon when it is used in construction. As the strength of a wall depends on its ability to act as an integral unit, so its weight gives stability to the horizontal lines that run through it.

The conventional size of a brick is based on the builder's need to handle it easily. Consequently, the scale of a brick wall's pattern is directly connected to the size of a hand, and, whether we realize it or not, the relationship of our bodies to its proportions. When a larger element such as a concrete block is used, the scale of the wall changes; this often occurs on a large or important building, when the scale of the block is increased. The classic form of an arch uses the forces of compression to stay intact and can thus span great distances with brick.

Concrete is is inherently strong in compression. It is heavy, like stone, and is normally reinforced with steel to help resist tension. Both marble and stone have a tactile nature which is as important as their figuring. Large quantites of either can change the acoustics in a room; this can either be enjoyed or reduced with the introduction of soft materials such as fabrics or rugs.

159

LEFT **A distressed wooden cupboard reflects the natural themes of a simple country kitchen. The varied** greens of the ceramic tiles behind continue the associations of the outdoor world and bounce daylight back into the room beyond.

a mellow, idiosyncratic look to the design. Ageing furniture needs to be introduced with discretion, however, as revealed by the dresser on page 157, slowly but gracefully loosing the battle to keep its paint. The contrast with the clean surrounding walls directs attention to the texture of the dresser, but the impact would be lost in a room full of simulated antique objects.

An illusion of light and space can also be achieved by a judicious selection of materials. The light coloured ceramic tiles above the dresser shown here, for example, are ideal for a kitchen, reflecting light and heat away from traditional stoves and bringing a more balanced, cooler feel to a busy space. Materials are at least partially responsible for light lev-

els in a room, and ceramic tiles may introduce notes of warmth or coolness, depending on their colour and finish.

The attraction of the finish of some materials can be in the way they wear their own history. As any material ages, it acquires a patina of grime, with corresponding lighter areas where it has worn most. Dark, worn wood reveals its legacy of domestic experience in a particularly special way. The low-lit, complex series of rooms illustrated opposite and on pages 158–9 use texture to demarcate areas of the house, mingling wooden boards and textured matting, cool flagstones and rich rugs. Strongly defined door frames are reinforced by adjacent rectangular hangings, pictures and reliefs or are occasionally softened by

heavy curtain fabric. The sombre rooms are enlivened by touches of metal, marbling and mock stone columns, whilst low reliefs break up the smooth texture of the walls without losing the house's somewhat mysterious, historic feel.

BARING THE BONES

Where materials used in the structure of a building – such as stone, wood, brick, metals and concrete – are introduced into decorative schemes inside it, the effect can transform our conventional perception of inside and out. This can be seen to dramatic effect in contemporary buildings constructed with the international materials of iron, steel, chrome and aluminium. For more traditional buildings, locally sourced materials – the yellow sandstone of the Cotswolds or slate in Wales are well-known examples – can be used inside as well as out as a way of emphasizing a building's sense of belonging within its location.

Decades before the Pompidou Centre in Paris was built, the influential American architect Louis Sullivan reversed the normal relationship of structures and frames in the Guaranty Building in Buffalo, N.Y. The external aspect of this large office block is dominated by a sleek

KEYNOTES

- STRUCTURE

- PROPORTION

- AUTHENTICITY

- BALANCING COLOUR

- REFLECTION

- ABSORPTION

- COMPLEMENTS AND CONTRASTS

Wood is one of the most versatile building materials and responds well to a range of treatments and finishes. The dark, polished patina of an antique bed or intricately carved cupboard bring powerful resonance to a traditional interior. Although all kinds of wood are now available, the individual types retain very specific identities and associations with the regions where they are grown.

and elegant steel frame. 'External' materials, such as glass, chrome and stainless steel, have become popular in modern design schemes because they bring light into a space without glare. In the sleek living room pictured below, the pale reflective colours of floor and walls increase the feeling of light. Complementary warm colours and matt texture of the artworks and furniture prevent a

serene atmosphere from becoming cold. Our current fondness for using such 'honest' materials indoors has developed because we admire their cool, clean, efficient properties, derived through our association of their use in an industrial environment. There is also a sneaking suspicion that by bringing them into our homes, we somehow hope that they will make us cool, clean and efficient too.

The clean lines and reflective surfaces of modern materials adapt well to a neutral, contemporary design. A double layer of thick, milky glass has been used to divide this open-plan kitchen from the sitting area without diminishing the sense of space. A free-standing stainless steel sink unit reflects light from its curved shiny surface into the room.

NEW, HARD MATERIALS AND TEXTURES

*From innovative plastics to stone, wood and iron,
hard materials are essential elements of design*

Radiators, once considered a
functional detail to be concealed,
are now a feature of many designs.
They may be outlined on domestic
walls like works of art or introduced
as coiled steel springs in sculptural
shapes. Others provide exuberant
focal points in brightly coloured,
high gloss paint.

USING HARDWARE

The underlying structures of our homes
are composed of hard materials that
exert a powerful influence on domestic
design. Many of the most exciting new
materials – plastics, perspex, chrome
and wire – are sophisticated forms of
hardware that challenge any conventional division between utilitarian and
decorative use. Others – the staples of
brick, slate, plaster, glass, iron and steel
– have dominated homes since the
Industrial Revolution and often before,
yet their more durable modern counterparts offer potential for innovation and
greater flexibility. Tempered glass,
strong enough to withstand human
weight, enables us to have larger, safer
windows. Better protective treatments
for timber and metal fittings means that
they require less maintenance and can be
more clearly displayed. Yet hardware has
always inspired radical interpretations.
The sinuous, fluid designs of Art Nouveau lamps, furniture and fittings
changed contemporary perceptions of
iron, bronze, glass and ceramics as
powerfully as cable and aluminium
structures have done for us today.

BALANCING HARD MATERIALS

Whilst certain hard materials seem to be
a miracle of science, others retain a sense
of the earth in both texture and tone.
Brick, stone, marble, slate and ceramics
reflect the earth's colour palette of greys,

RIGHT **The reflective quality of the copper cladding on the wooden steps of this narrow staircase is** strengthened by the addition of narrow tubes of lights beneath each step. Their soft and welcoming glow complements the cool white wall behind the stairs.

BELOW **Metals can also work well over large areas if carefully integrated into the scheme. A bank of** textured metal doors provides a dramatic wall treatment, cleverly concealing a set of floor to ceiling cupboards. Two angular metal chairs extend the industrial theme into the bright room beyond.

LEFT **The distinctive textures of ceramic and stone can introduce a subtle change of mood within a** design. A beautifully turned, crackle-glazed pot is displayed on a surface of rich earth tones, while a large beach pebble provides an unexpectedly tactile handle to a sleek painted door.

browns, rich ochres and creams, providing an intriguing anchor to hi-tech design schemes. The diverse character of hard materials brings a stimulus and focus to their juxtaposition, particularly in unexpected settings.

We need to free ourselves of the preconceived belief that certain materials are only appropriate for certain jobs. This is particularly true of the softer, non-ferrous metals, such as copper and aluminium, available in many different finishes and shapes. Traditionally used as a roofing material that will oxidize to a distinctive blue-green, copper is also commonly found in the decoration and plumbing of our homes. In the sleek staircase shown above left, it is used to face the risers of the stairs, thus introducing a warm, reflective quality to the space. The reflection is accentuated by the linear lighting positioned just under the overhang, or nosing. This design is both attractive and practical, allowing safer use of the stairway in the dark.

Iron and steel are commonly used in the construction of buildings, bolted, riveted or welded together to form the skeletal cage, or framework. However, they can bring dramatic focus to interior spaces, both as details, such as curtain poles and finials, and as features extending over a larger area. Even a relatively traditional space can accommodate small accents for textural contrast.

Although functional metals are conventionally considered to be industrial materials, we are now beginning to use them to add a different texture and dimension to domestic areas. In new buildings, extruded metal sections are often used as decorative elements such as skirting and architrave. Rolled steel sheets can be treated with all kinds of effects, from being squeezed through textured rollers to controlled chemical attack, to provide them with an interesting texture. When you are combining hard materials, it is very important to try to judge the balance of one material against another – cool against warm, matt against reflective. The materials will relate differently according to the space, depending on its light, size, colour and furnishings. In the contemporary, angular room opposite, the warm, honey coloured wood flooring is juxtaposed with cool, contrasting aluminium panels. These provide reflection and establish a grid, bringing a rhythm to the room. The deep skirting, painted in white, helps the balance and adds strength to the floor.

Polished wooden boxes, a ceramic dish and an elegantly shaped piece of lacquerware provide an interesting assortment of materials in a neutrally toned space. The combination of smooth lines, curves and grooves creates a balanced and harmonious arrangement.

The way in which two different textures interact is not dissimilar to the way colours work together. We may be right when we say that old brick and polished steel look good when viewed next to one another. We need to consider how textures will be seen in the context of the whole room and measure the proportion of one material against the other to ensure that a balance is maintained.

Conservatories, constructed from glass, place the structural framework uniquely on display – decoration does itself comprise the structure, and vice versa. Brass, bronze, nickel and satin-chrome can bring gleaming colour and texture to fittings. Light gauge steel, once it has been treated to prevent corrosion, is a practical, light-enhancing material for window fittings, channels and ducting, as well as for decorative

The unexpected use of high-tension cable has produced a dark, highly textured wall feature. The twists of the cable establish a rhythm and pattern that has a curiously relaxing effect when viewed close up. The variation of texture sets up an interesting play of light, so the wall, although dense, is not perceived as uniform or static.

details. Iron, beloved by the early industrial age, can be moulded into a wide range of forms and shapes, from solid girders to the delicate tracery of ornamental baskets and furniture. The sense of touch is extremely important in our awareness of materials, and the cool, smooth surfaces of metals invite physical contact. They work well as a counterbalance to the rougher textures of stone or brick, which can in turn bring a rich, warm tone to floors, walls or accessories.

Stone is firmly anchored to its origins in the earth, carrying associations of the natural world into an interior environment. The variety of stone colours, and their impact on a space, needs to be carefully considered in the context of the whole room. Slate, for example, may be grey-green or mottled, with attractive streaks of rust; sandstone exists in cream, grey or buff forms, and their surfaces may be rustic or honed smooth, absorbing or reflecting light. The main weaknesses of stone lie in stain and wear – porous stones, such as limestone, will require a sealant to avoid staining as water is absorbed – and in weight. Stone tiled floors in bathrooms can certainly look sensational, but will the joists of an upper storey take the strain?

Stone also works well as small, decorative detail, especially in an unusual context. The door knob pictured on page 165, made from a large beach pebble, offers a contrast of shape and texture in a smooth, linear space and invites touch. Such small details gain strength and impact if repeated throughout the space, changing our perception of the material and its connotations.

TEXTURE AND ILLUSION

Materials may be adapted to suit a wide variety of domestic locations. They can create interesting illusions of perspective within a room, particularly where there is little other structural interest. The very special feature wall illustrated here, made from lengths of high-tension cable, seizes the attention and dominates a modern living room. The repeated lengths of horizontal cable expand the room's sense of width and create a rich texture onto which light can be played. The dark matt wall also appears to recede from the eye, giving a feeling of depth to the room beyond its very ordinary shape. Warm tones in the rug help to soften the contrast between the white sofas and dark grey wall, as do the elaborate bamboo chairs.

Illusion is not confined to new materials, however; more conventional ones, such as plaster and concrete, may also determine our perceptions of a space. Plaster can be made to appear crumbling in order to complement distressed paint finishes and create interesting textural variation. Even the much maligned contrete can be used in imaginative ways. A poured material, it will assume the texture of whatever has been used as a mould to form it, even achieving a resemblance to wood and steel. The slabs used to construct London's National Theatre were formed using rough sawn planking, so that the saw marks and grain, as well as the offset planks, give an interesting, haphazard texture to the sur-

face. The size of the planks also gives the viewer a scale with which to read the building in its large, open context.

Architects have been fascinated for centuries by the way in which light plays on surfaces, and textured concrete offers a modern interpretation of the different effects that can be achieved. New techniques of illumination, such as washing and grazing walls with light (see page 95), can only add to the opportunities for dramatic textural highlights.

WORKING WITH WOOD

Wood is perhaps the most versatile of hard materials in its response to different finishes. Whether it is lacquered, painted or polished, it can have a surprisingly

ABOVE **This simple bedroom at Pope Leighey, Virginia was designed by the architect Frank Lloyd Wright.** Dominated by wood, it emphasizes natural markings and grains as part of the material's authenticity. The polished, reflective surfaces draw daylight into the room and prevent the mood becoming overly sombre.

RIGHT **The bathroom in Lloyd Wright's home at Oak Park, Illinois also features wood strongly in** structure and decoration. Designed by Lloyd Wright, it is a functional, focused space in which the horizontal wooden planks are balanced by the lighter colour of the upper walls and ceiling. A woven wool rug softens the floor without detracting from the room's calm simplicity.

KEYNOTES

- REFLECTION
- INNOVATION
- HARMONY AND RHYTHM
- ACCENTS
- HORIZONTALS AND VERTICALS
- ATMOSPHERE
- LIGHT AND SPACE

Playing with the grain of a wood can create interesting effects, without the need for paint. The wood panelling in this bathroom forms a design of alternate dark and pale stripes, co-ordinating with the dark slate surfaces around washbasin and bath.

powerful impact on a room – whether traditional or contemporary in style – without losing its own identity. Rooms designed by Frank Lloyd Wright, shown on the two preceding pages, place a characteristic emphasis on simple wood panelling and paint colours. They reveal the extent to which wood can reinforce its associations with the natural world.

The choice of wood type and the direction of its grain contribute to the atmosphere of a room. If the grain and colour are constant and without figuring, then the space will appear to be calmer than it will if there is more variation in the wood. Comparison of the bathroom illustrated on the previous page with the one above demonstrates

that, while each is panelled, different woods can create significantly different effects. The first bathroom has been panelled to a picture rail height with horizontal planks of a dark matt wood, with a consistent horizontal grain. It produces a calm atmosphere in the space and emphasizes the room's width. In contrast, the strongly figured grain in the wood-finished bathroom shown above has created a bright, vibrant mood. This has been accentuated in turn by the ceiling to sink-top mirror and low-voltage recessed downlighting. In the latter case, the direction of the grain has been used to increase a sense of height in the room, and to add some contrasting texture amongst plain and shiny surfaces.

USING SOFTER, ORGANIC MATERIALS

Carefully crafted natural textures bring refreshing accents and definition to contemporary design

Natural materials work well as small decorative details, providing textural contrast to an overall design. Their fresh, homespun associations are particularly appropriate for culinary items, such as these attractive cruet coverings.

NATURAL MATERIALS

Materials described as organic share a strong identification with the natural world. In contrast to the highly wrought forms of many materials, organic ones still bear the character of the plant – or animal – from which they were derived. Ranging from wicker and rattan to leather, sea grass and cotton, organic materials work well as contemporary details, accents or striking keynotes in a design. While they bring an informal, more relaxed note to an interior scheme – and adapt well to natural colour tones and light, simply furnished spaces – organic materials also possess a sharpness of texture that stops a neutral space from becoming bland. As well as celebrating our own rural heritage, we also have access to more exotic ingredients from other cultures: abaca or banana fibre, sisal and jute, rich Indian dhurries and elegant bamboo.

TEXTURES AND TREATMENTS

Some organic materials are naturally hard wearing, whereas others require special treatment or care. Despite their apparent simplicity, some can be quite complex to maintain and it is important to consider practical as well as aesthetic requirements. Traditionally associated with homely, rural design themes, the impression of longevity, of being worn through use, is part of their enjoyed effect. Apparent age may be genuine – perhaps the sign of an inherited piece that has accrued value over generations – or simulated by techniques of antiquing and distressing. Natural materials such as wood and bamboo (which, despite its strength and appearance, is actually a grass, not a wood) can be treated with wax or oil as they age to develop an attractive patina or depth.

Leather, now available in many forms, from traditional buttoned upholstery to more contemporary woven panels, will also mellow – some say improve – over time. It needs to be cleaned and fed to remain supple, but such care will bring the rewards of textural contrast and a luxurious aroma to a room. Although traditionally considered an upholstery fabric, leather provides an attractive, if expensive, floor or wall treatment. It also enables us to manipulate the play of light by choosing one of a number of the surface finishes available that offer different levels of sheen. Suede, for example, can be used to introduce leather to a scheme in its matt form. Suede is a much warmer material to the touch and will also tend to show its colour off better than polished leather. A sustainable and attractive material, it is very hard wearing, providing it is properly protected

171

Painted wood has a softer impact
on a scheme than in its untreated
form. This gently peeling cupboard
with natural, muted colour tones
provides attractive but unobtrusive
storage for a collection of antique
porcelain and glass.

change our perception of rattan, wicker and, particularly, wood. It turns such materials from the rustic to the strategically honed, even changing our perception of their shape by making them appear larger when painted in light, reflective hues and sharper and slimmer in dark matt colours.

THE AUTHENTIC LOOK

Despite the sophistication of materials such as polished leather and rubber, a rural, hand-crafted look remains the key theme of many organic materials. Natural fabrics, such as wool, silk, cotton and linen, are made directly from renewable natural fibres (see page 200). The inconsistencies in quality that are sometimes found in their textures can add to the character of a design scheme.

Traditionally, functional cottons and linens were embellished by braid trimmings or tassels that are still consistent with their homespun mood. These authentic, comfortable fabrics can be adapted into a design in various ways. Stiffened cotton makes effective blinds to protect privacy and keep temperatures down in bright sunlight. Delicate voile or muslin sheers, or gossamer-thin cotton awnings, soften and diffuse the

against dirt and stains, and introduces a feeling of quality to a space. It works well on a small scale or as an accent: suede or polished leather cushions, for example, bring textural and thematic contrast to a fabric sofa.

Paint remains one of the simplest finishing treatments for organic materials. Used over large or small surfaces, it can

LEFT **The contrasting patterns of individual weaves provide eye-catching details within a design.** Tightly woven or more open for a lacy, netted effect, they work well as decorative borders on blinds, cushions, tablelinen and throws.

RIGHT **This crisp, two-tone linen cushion uses smooth, reflective buttons to provide a local contrast** to its smart look. Their shiny, reflective surface works well against the closely woven matt fabric.

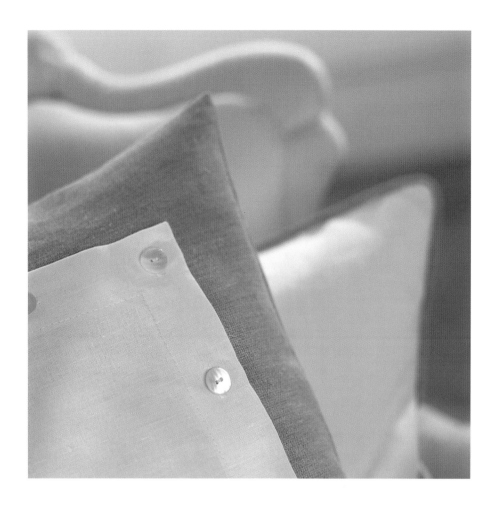

BELOW **Embroidery, crewel work, appliqué and needlepoint are traditional ways of introducing** new colour and texture to a fabric. Practical as well as decorative, raised motifs can distract attention from worn corners of an antique piece of furniture such as this highly polished chair.

natural light in a room, whilst they retain an attractive freedom of movement. Sheers should be white in order to achieve a natural light effect, but a gentle pastel shade will create delicately shifting pools of colour on the walls and floor. Alternatively, choose a range of colours that will reflect the light – and moods – of the changing seasons.

Paper can be used as a window treatment material to enhance delicate, translucent schemes and to introduce a note of oriental refinement into a Western home. A more complete shade from the sun is provided by resilient pinoleum blinds, which are made from pine reeds woven with cotton yarn with a tough, polyester core. Such discreet manmade additions have dramatically improved the practicality and durability of organic fabrics without compromising their authentic, ethnic feel.

KEYNOTES

• TEXTURE AND PATTERN

• AUTHENTICITY

• NATURAL COLOURS

• PRACTICALITY

• PRESERVATION

• HARMONY AND BALANCE

• ASSOCIATION

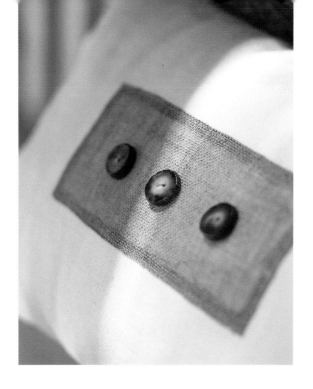

LEFT Linen is a very versatile fabric which can be adopted into many interior schemes. Its weight and structure make it a good choice for curtains and upholstery, but it also brings a crispness to soft cushion forms. A smart geometric panel and decorative buttons bring a touch of sophistication to this simple shape.

RIGHT The ordered, slightly oriental pattern of this woollen rug is created from the texture of the fabric itself. Attractive and adaptable, wool provides a good base material for floor treatments; it may then be juxtaposed with the more abrasive jute or sisal, or with exposed and sanded boards.

NATURAL FLOORING

The hard-wearing properties – or otherwise – of natural materials are particularly important if they are used for floors. The rough-hewn, gently abrasive textures of abaca, jute, sea grass and sisal accommodate most design schemes and provide a good foil for wooden furniture and fitments. A number of floor coverings today are made from bamboo, traditionally split and woven into baskets but for this purpose cut and bonded into sheet form. Like all matt surfaces, they absorb rather than reflect light, providing a useful anchor for natural colour schemes of ecru, whites, buffs and browns. In a kitchen, hallway, conservatory or other tiled area, natural floor covering can provide a useful textural complement to stone flags or cool tiles – and a valuable means of introducing a sense of calm in sometimes busy or congested areas. That said, while some can be used successfully in unfitted form in kitchens, most natural floorings are generally unsuitable for bathrooms. This is because if grass-based materials come into contact with water, they will attempt to shrink or stretch back to their original state, prior to the manufacturing processes of drying and weaving. It is particularly true of sea grass or sisal flooring, which expand if wet and retain stains. (Rush matting, on the other hand, is unique in actually needing water to retain its suppleness – a watering can, rather than a vacuum cleaner, is important for its care.) Rich, textured rugs and dhurries can provide an attractive alternative for cold bathroom floors, however, and there are now a number of wool-mix carpets available to resemble the less stable natural floor cooverings.

Wool carpet, once dismissed in contemporary schemes as too traditional, in fact has more diversity than it is normally given credit for. It can also integrate well with most classic or contemporary design themes. From various expensive, high-quality ranges like the woven Axminsters and Wiltons to cheaper glued, tufted versions, wool carpets offer the sensation of a natural fibre as well as resilience, longevity and the joy of being easy to maintain. When combined with a small percentage of artificial fibre, they also offer excellent durability. The density of a wool carpet is the key to its performance – the more dense it is, the less inclined its tufts will be to lie flat when trampled and thus age prematurely. Wool carpet also has a versatility that accommodates degrees of colour complexity, borders and even scupltured patterns of the kind featured opposite. These qualities can offer either subtle or more dominant textural layers to work with the lighting schemes, shape and decoration of a particular space.

ACCENTS AND DETAILS

Organic materials in a harmonious overall scheme can provide intriguing contrasts of texture, shape and theme. Accents and accessories are often the best way to introduce complementary elements, including those not normally thought of as ingredients of domestic design. Shells, coral, pebbles and even bone can provide very personal still-lifes in a bathroom or hallway, perhaps offset by glass or a dark, polished wood. Individual frames made from bark or splintered driftwood form a bold demarcation between the smooth surface of wall and the painting or photograph displayed. Fruit, too, is highly decorative in a pot pourri arrangement of nuts, feathers and architectural seed heads of poppy or teasel. Almost all textures and colours of the natural world will work well with organic materials in an original, contemporary setting.

MIXING AND
MATCHING
MATERIALS

Juxtaposing materials with different
characteristics enhances our perceptions of each

COMPLEMENTARY MATERIALS

The variety of domestic materials has
increased dramatically in recent years,
from rediscovered ethnic products to
newly applied plastics, metals and glass.
However, although their different
shapes and colours may complement
each other well in an interior, the real
value of these new-found materials lies
in their textural contrast. This is particularly true in a monochromatic scheme,
where variations in texture achieve
greater impact when colour is pared
back. Textural contrast should not be a
reaction to a fear of colour, however, but
an ingredient working along with, and as
part of, the existing scheme. Combinations of cool and warm, hard and soft,
rough and smooth, are useful in grouping different items, but need to be
carefully thought out. If a contrast is
struck in texture, colour or shape, for
example, then the other elements of the
room should work together to provide a
balance. If all the features of a space contrast, the discord is unbearable.

Contrasting materials work well as
keynote features and as details, but it is
perhaps as accessories that they really
come into their own. Whether they are
personal momentoes or classic objects of

desire, accessories introduce textural
notes that can either work with a theme
or in contrast to it. The shape of a relatively small-scale object will often have a
great impact, especially if it is imaginatively displayed. Venetian glass, ceramics
and porcelain, for example, can all bring
light to a space because of their reflective
surfaces and help to counter dark, non-
reflective textures such as aged wood.
They will also pick up light from a paler
surface and reflect it into the room, making the space feel more airy and alive.
Smooth, clean surfaces can give an
importance to objects with tactile textures, such as carved wood, coarse and
embroidered textiles or arrangements of
shells or pebbles.

Such juxtapositions can be particularly effective in situations where they
subtly challenge a prevailing scheme.
The yellow of a natural sponge and the
soft natural fibres of a loofah, for example, will help to make a bathroom feel
less clinical and more comfortable. The
gentler mood can be further enhanced
by an imaginative selection of materials
for essential appliances. Brass taps on
the bathroom fittings, for example, will
create a warm glow that chrome simply
cannot achieve.

LEFT **This harmonious bedroom reveals a clever combination of materials. The crisp linen texture of** bed cover and co-ordinated scatter cushions is balanced with a simple wooden bench at the foot of the bed and the honey-coloured headboard against the wall. A complex mixture of shape and scale, the room retains coherence through the strength of the underlying natural theme.

KEYNOTES

- COOLNESS AND WARMTH

- SHAPE AND FORM

- VERTICALS AND HORIZONTALS

- PERSPECTIVE

- TEXTURAL CONTRAST

- NATURAL COLOURS

- ANTIQUE AND MODERN

BALANCING TEXTURES

We are, logically, more likely to find soft materials in the areas of our homes where we relax or sleep than in the functional regions of a kitchen or bathroom. Nevertheless, the cooler and harder textures of wood, stone or gleaming metal can often be used in such areas to offset softly draped fabrics and create useful focal points. The use of complementary shape helps to preserve the balance between contrasting textures, as can be seen in the carefully proportioned wall weave set against a smooth backdrop above. The neat cornice and simple door act as a foil for the over-sized bed-head in this cool, understated bedroom. The surfaces around the bed are soft and

rounded, contrasting with the linear bedside light and the minimal bench at the end of the bed. A balance is maintained, and the relationship of hard and soft textures, sharp and rounded shapes, focuses attention on the bed. This is all contained within a soft, monotone scheme that allows materials and textures to dominate over colour.

It is obviously important to consider the practical properties of a material, but equally we need to be able to use it imaginatively. In the elegant dining space illustrated opposite, the celebrated architect Le Corbusier married strong and unexpected materials, and in doing so challenged our perceptions of the room. The warm brick of the barrel-

vaulted ceiling heats up the cool marble table, which has been placed to reflect daylight from the courtyard beyond. Meanwhile, the lines of perspective set up by the ceiling bricks are counter-balanced by the horizontal wrought iron ties running across it. The curve of the warm coloured ceiling is in contrast to the rigid block fireplace in the centre of the room, but echoes the rounded leather chairs and helps soften the hard, linear materials in the room. The choice of materials is both sensible and practical, but the secret of this dining room lies in their highly considered juxtaposition and in the relationship that is achieved between the shapes of the structure and of the furniture.

SUSPENDED SPACE

Combinations of hard materials such as glass, wrought iron and other metals with softer fabrics and rugs can work well to suit a variety of spaces. One of the most interesting in textural terms is the conservatory, a space suspended between house and garden which opens its doors to textures of brick, stone and stucco to reinforce its exterior connection. These are unique 'garden rooms', in which structural elements are constantly on display, tempered by the organic associations of wicker, rattan, sisal and linen. The 'bones' of a conservatory are revealed in fixtures and fittings of brass, iron or bronze, which can be echoed by decorative wirework in the form of trellis or baskets. Even in the floor, complementary textures emerge,

The linear effect of this living area designed by Le Corbusier is emphasized by the combination of materials featured in its interior. Cool marble and smooth leather are counterpointed by the warm red tones of the vaulted brick ceiling. Shapes – for example, the curved ceiling structure and the backs of the dining chairs – also echo and cross-refer to one another.

Good design is also sustenance. What we create now

is destined to feed or starve future generations

LEFT AND BELOW **It is not necessary to isolate more abrasive textured fabrics. By juxtaposing a rattan** cushion with a luxurious length of velvet, or a rough slub linen with sleek satin, we can bring stimulating focal points into a design.

RIGHT **The influence of ethnic cultures, particularly those of the East, has changed the look of** many contemporary interiors. Western antique furniture, such as this aged leather armchair, can now exist harmoniously with Chinese paint pots, plus a bamboo ladder and plant.

in the form of iron grilles for underfloor heating, juxtaposed with stone and ceramic tiles and woven wool rugs.

Glass dominates many modern rooms, most of all conservatories whose walls are essentially picture windows on the outside world. New technology has produced safety glass which can be used in larger panes, and a form of low-emissivity glass that reflects heat back into the room from a virtually invisible coating. Glass has also become more popular for fixtures and fittings, and for use in stairs, floors and walls. It can be curved and moulded into a huge range of decorative forms and given a variety of tints, colours and finishes to control its interaction with other materials. By

enabling us to see objects from different angles, it emphasizes how the position of items makes us respond to them in a different way. For example, if you placed a roughly textured material next to a highly polished marble, the textured surface would appear more textured and the marble more polished as a result.

CREATING CONTRASTS

As materials become more sophisticated, it is important not to become overwhelmed by illusion and artifice. The beliefs of the early 20th-century German architect Ludwig Mies van der Rohe that there should be an honesty and integrity in the use of materials, and that function should determine form, are

points to consider when shaping our own designs. Mies van der Rohe essentially believed in selecting the most appropriate material for the task in hand and letting it speak for itself, not smothered with pastiche or unsuitable companions that disturb its integrity.

It is important to understand the keynotes for schemes featuring contrasting materials, wherever they occur. The chair with woven leather straps illustrated above highlights the differing textures produced by weaves. Smooth leather contrasts with soft rich corduroy in a cushion and is supported by the tightly woven matting or another. It also works well with the grain of the floor and the smooth wall behind.

MATERIALS AND FURNITURE

Furniture can redefine the impact of a room through its shape, size, material and position

RIGHT The smooth dark leather of these two Barcelona chairs designed by Mies van der Rohe is well defined against the pale wood of the floor and strong texture of the rug. The positioning of furniture changes our perception of every-thing around it and dominant pieces should be placed with care. In this room the chairs form a focal point and determine the use and flow of the space around them.

FORM AND FUNCTION

One of the most powerful ways of introducing a theme and sense of place to a room is through furniture and accessories. Ideally, these should reflect existing shapes, structures and patterns and the significance of each piece be understood in terms of a room's focus and balance. Large pieces give a scheme a strength and sense of purpose (hence the designer's fondness for using a few pieces of 'over-sized' furniture) and should be used to dominate; smaller pieces can then provide subtle accents.

The balance of furniture can greatly contribute to the mood of a room: the less furniture there is, the greater impact it has on perspective and atmosphere. Too often we cram our rooms with furniture we do not really need, and in doing so create confusion between the different elements of a design. Remember that our perception of a basic form is always influenced by its material. Identically shaped chairs or tables will have a presence that depends upon the materials from which they are made – say, iron, plastic or wood – and will also evoke very different associations. Colour and texture also affect how furniture is viewed in its setting; brightly coloured

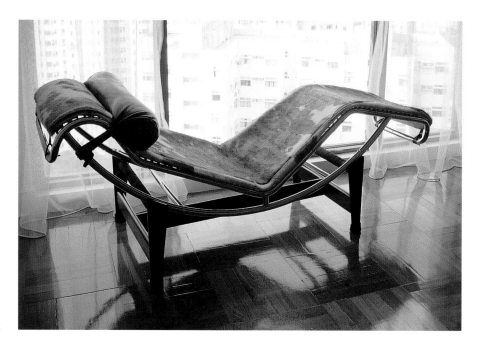

items provide a natural focal point and should be chosen with an eye to balance and proportion within the room. In a more minimalist scheme, however, contrast and pattern will rely less on colour than on texture.

EXPLORING TEXTURE AND SHAPE

The texture of a piece of furniture defines or softens our perception of its shape and determines its relationship with colours and surfaces in a room.

ABOVE The sculptured frame of this elegant Le Corbusier 'lounge chair' is made from chrome tubular steel. It provides harmonious contrast with the soft textural suede of the chair covering. The shape itself plays with conventional proportions, holding a long back and smooth curves in equilibrium; its silhouette against the window appears to float above the reflective floor.

The material and texture of furniture can continue a design scheme on from one room to another, or indeed from inside to outside. This is particularly the case with furniture used in porches or conservatories – both areas that have close relationships with the garden beyond. Furniture made from wicker – cut and woven willow shoots – and rattan cane is not only useful by being strong and lightweight, but strengthens the correspondences between indoors and out through its clearly organic nature. Open wicker armchairs, complemented by bamboo-cane side tables, are often used for such spaces, as well as in

RIGHT **A simple dining area successfully combines a variety of different materials. The rustic** wooden table draped with linen is placed upon floor covering of natural fibre. Carefully mismatched chairs in wood, plastic and metal bring an imaginative focus to the scene.

constant repetition of a line, for example, emphasizes an item's length. The contemporary chair shown above uses the material from which it is constructed for practical and aesthetic effect. Woven cane provides the piece's substance and reveals its shape and form through the geometry of the weave. The striking unity of the chair's curving form gives it a sense of solidity and support.

Such a technique is not confined to modern furnishings, however. By using a tailored corduroy as an upholstery material, the rounded Edwardian sofa pictured opposite has been given a crisper, more defined form.

functional rooms such as bathrooms and kitchens that benefit from association with the natural world.

Contemporary furniture offers a wide range of possibilities, not least because there are so many materials and designs from which to choose. They may be comfortable and anchoring or frivolous and light-hearted; perspex items, for example, will tease our instinctive perception of solids and light. Many of the imaginative styles and materials in today's furniture arose during a period of creative experiment in the early 20th century. Newly available chrome, plated steel and tubular aluminium were fea-

tures of designs that celebrated the aesthetics of mass-production. The famous 'lounge chair' of Le Corbusier, illustrated on page 186, would fit happily into a contemporary loft; it was actually created in 1928 and features modern materials well engineered to cope with the stresses of daily use. Like Mies van der Rohe's cantilevered steel chairs, shown on the preceding page and designed in 1929, it complements and contrast with the colours and textures of floors and walls.

Against the school of furniture design powered by new, industrial materials, the distinctive clean lines and geometric

Many manmade fabrics have a pile and an obvious design direction which make them well suited for upholstering furniture. This curvaceous sofa has gained a more tailored appearance and crispness of line by the sharp stripe of the cord defining its shape.

shapes of the Wiener Werkstätte were unconventional ways of using more conventional materials. Celebrating individual craftsmanship above mass-produced design, this group of Viennese artists and designers drew upon the ideas of William Morris and John Ruskin to create harmonious, imaginative items for domestic use. Many of them have now become design classics.

COMBINING STYLES

A good deal of contemporary furniture is available that embraces both industrial and organic aesthetics. However, the problems many of us face when choosing furniture are how to create a modern look that is not too 'hard', or how to include older, perhaps inherited, pieces of furniture within an established contemporary design. It is important to remember that the boundaries between a 'period' or 'modern' look do not have to be as rigidly defined as we might think to create a visual coherence. Where a dilemma does exist, it may be resolved in part by careful positioning of items within the room, so that one particular piece does not stifle another, or by covering an antique chair, say, with a

BELOW Light and its many reflections emphasize the textural contrast of materials in a scheme. In this cool, elegant bathroom, the role of a faceted mirror is enhanced by the metallic chairs, chrome plumbing and silvered jug by the bath.

KEYNOTES

- COLOUR AND SHAPE

- CONTRASTING MATERIALS

- ENHANCING FORM

- PRACTICALITY

- REFLECTION

- ABSORPTION

- PROPORTION

more contemporary fabric. Different finishing techniques may also help by changing the emphasis or impact of a material whilst bringing an attractive new element into the design. The key is to forge visual relationships between the styles. The lines of both may be either strongly vertical or horizontal; each piece may be constructed of the same material or be of a toning colour.

Furniture, more than any other aspect of room design, has an intrinsic character. Whether they are arch or bold, flamboyant or unassuming, we should try to find pieces that project the same statement. Alternatively, we should look for furniture that will be naturally subservient to a scheme dominated by older, more powerfully designed pieces. This can be done by opting for simpler, less angular shapes that contain organic elements such as leather, wood or cotton in natural colours.

Tables and chairs are often one of the most difficult combinations of furniture to get right. The mixture of legs, for example, needs to be harmonious both in style and material, neither of which is easy to predict in isolation. Different tones of wood, for example, may not always work well together; sometimes

metal and wood, or metal and marble, may be more successful. Plastics are an obviously practical but also attractive material for an informal dining area, particularly if there is a matt texture in adjacent floor or walls to balance the brash colour. If the two seem impossible to match, remember that tables can be dressed with cloths and flowers to completely transform them.

Furniture has associations with time and place, and there is immense value in incorporating good quality antiques into even the most contemporary scheme. It engenders a sense of design for living and a continuity with earlier generations, and acknowledges an enduring quality and style beyond the reach of today's 'disposable' trends.

Kitchens often successfully combine a range of varied but complementary materials. A dark oak table co-ordinates with heavy beams in this rustic ceiling, yet remains at ease with the light coloured, free-standing work surface and cupboards that introduce a more modern atmosphere.

WALL
TREATMENTS

Paper and paint are not the only media to hand for introducing light and surface texture to walls

RIGHT **Square wood panels bring a protective feel to the sleeping area in this bright, modern bedroom.** Their polished surface allows some light from the downlit recesses to spill onto the bed, while the mirrored cupboard doors contribute to the reflection of light in the room.

WORKING THE WALLS

Far from being mere structural ingredients or passive receptors of whatever is hung on or placed against them, walls make a powerful contribution to our perception of a room. If covered in the wrong wallpaper or painted in an indifferent colour, they can appear to be no more than boundary markers, but by choosing the right treatment we can enhance the design and the atmosphere we seek to create.

When deciding how to treat a conventional interior wall, we should bear in mind the needs of the room itself. Its sound level, for example, will be dictated by the accoustic properties of the materials used. Soft, porous materials – such as tented ceilings and fabric covered walls, even heavy wallpapers – will absorb sound, while most hard surfaces (unless they have been specially engineered) will appear to increase its volume by bouncing it across the room.

Wall finishes can obviously affect the volume of light reflected within a space, which is why glass (though it is a high-maintenance material) can solve problems with dark spaces. A large mirror can create the effect of a complete glass wall and substantially influence

both light levels and the room's perceived size. If using it on this scale, however, reflections should be considered carefully, as any negative elements, such as an awkward feature or unattractive view, will have double the impact. Screens may also be constructed with glass bricks or panels, creating a demarcation without restricting the flow of light. A room with large amounts of glass will bring in not only an abundant daylight but also an open blackness at night, and can affect temperature and privacy.

No room is an island – each maintains some connection with the rest of the house or apartment. Think of the way your chosen treatment surrounds an open door and corresponds to the view of the room beyond. No wall will be smooth and continuous for long, even in a relatively large room, and the wall covering may need to accommodate some awkward corners and door frames. This could well be one good reason to reject a large patterned paper for use in a small space. Whatever treatment you choose, the extent of the wall covering should be thought about at an early stage, as continuity of materials, forms and colours on both walls and floors can expand the flow of space.

ABOVE **The natural feel of an interior dominated by different woods produces a mellow, harmonious** environment. The grain of the vertical wall panelling provides a clearly defined contrast to the mahogany cot bed and simple pine chest of drawers.

TREATMENTS AND FINISHES

By far the most common wall finish is paint. Flexible, versatile and economic, much of its effect is based on a spectrum of finishes that run from the soft, less durable and light-absorbing matt emulsions to the hard, highly reflective and durable enamels. Some of the premium paint manufacturers ensure that the number of pigments used to make up a colour will refract light, endowing some of the softer finishes with a degree of subtlety. However, we normally use a paint effect – that is, a number of thin-coloured glazes used one on top of the other – to provide depth to a surface. Stippling, colour washing, ragging and dragging, all effects that use one colour to part coat and part reveal a base coat of another, provide depth to a wall and create different moods. Coarsely colour washed walls in yellows and ochres give a hot, rustic feel, while finely stippled 'barely there' finishes in greens and greys give a refined airiness. A number of effects – notably wood-graining, marbling and stone blocking – engender atmosphere by means of imitation and often demand walls that are free of imperfection to manage the illusion.

BELOW **This free-standing bath is reflected in a floor to ceiling mirrored wall which exaggerates the** size of the room. Wallpaper should be introduced into a bathroom with caution to avoid any problems with condensation in a small area.

LEFT **Reflective surfaces are great assets in small rooms; in a bathroom they need to be functional as** well. This imaginative scheme places a steel washbasin against one completely mirrored wall, reflecting light from the ceiling spots. The gloss effect produced by a mosaic of tiny blue tiles transforms our perception of the space.

BELOW **If space is at a premium, a simple paint treatment is the best option. The low ceiling height of** this attic bathroom is maximized by washing the walls in a pale blue and keeping a single row of tiles to act as a splashback around the bath and washbasin.

Wallpaper can imitate, too, with wood, stone and reed effects; it is infinitely more versatile than paint because it offers more in the way of texture. Fabric, wood veneer, reeds, cotton fibres (flock) can all be paper-backed and mounted. And yet the value of this wall treatment continues to lie in an almost unending gallery of two-dimensional designs that provide a subtle foil or make a bold statement in a more neutral space. Wallpaper may establish the character of a room quickly and at relatively low cost, but its impact can be dramatic and sometimes unexpected. The colour and strength of a pattern can heavily influence a room's dimensions, lighting and balance of colour. It will also exacerbate wall irregularities and shape, particularly in the case of geometrics.

Heavily textured walls are one of the oldest forms of decorative treatment. Wool tapestries were originally functional items, hung to provide protection from draughts. Our contemporary interpretations of these, including dhurries, kilims, elaborate quilts and even silks, continue to bring a protective sense of warmth and enclosure. They can also serve as a visual 'anchor' to balance the flow of activity in dynamic regions of a

195

KEYNOTES

- PERSPECTIVE
- CONTINUITY AND DIVISION
- PATTERN AND TEXTURE
- RHYTHM
- RECEDING COLOURS
- ADVANCING COLOURS
- LIGHT AND SHADOW

RIGHT **Together with** *trompe l'oeil* **paintwork, hand-blocked wall-papers by French manufacturers** such as Zuber enjoyed great popularity in the late 18th and early 19th centuries. The scenes of romance and adventure shown in this example were typical of the French style.

BELOW **A different perspective of a hallway can be gained by covering the walls with trellis. This produces** an intriguing three-dimensional illusion and a focus of visual interest within a relatively narrow space.

house, such as stairs and hallways. Alternatively, they can introduce a bold display of colour and movement to a more static space. Organic wall weaves of cane or grasses, on the other hand, can bring a textural counterpoint to smooth, cool, walls. It is important to keep wall hangings in proportion to the room, or they may reduce light levels and induce a sense of claustrophobia.

Plaster as a wall finish originated in the warm Mediterranean climate, where the dry air helped to preserve decorative frescoes for centuries. While commonly used as a draught and sound insulating base for paint or paper finishes, many contemporary designs have left its rich texture exposed, recognizing how suc-

cessfully it responds to artifical light. When dyed with pigment and sealed, plaster carries an extraordinary interest and depth.

The cool, reflective qualities of ceramic tiles as a wall treatment have long been a feature of Moorish interiors. Their value extends beyond that of a water-resistant finish to providing a strong visual and textural accent. This contrasts well with natural textures such as rough-hewn stone, matt fabrics, rich brick or woven sisal or rattan floors. In large areas of solid colour, take care that grouted intersections of wall tiles do not contrast too heavily, as a large expanse of any repetitive pattern can prove mesmerizing rather than relaxing.

A SUMMARY OF **THE ESSENTIALS**

An holistic approach to design recognizes that we tend to be happiest in places whose design works in harmony with nature.

STRUCTURE

DURABILITY

REFLECTION

ABSORPTION

TRANSPARENCY

INNOVATION

BALANCE

FINISH

ACCENTS

HARMONY

197

5

FABRICS AND PATTERN

Fabric is an essential ingredient in an interior scheme. Set against harder materials, it provides a soft, forgiving element not only in its texture but in the fluidity of its line. Whether densely woven and opaque or the subtlest of sheers, fabrics determine the quantity and quality of light and influence the atmosphere and themes of a room. They also contribute much of the interest in a room through colour, texture and pattern. Not only associated with fabric, the variety of motifs and media through which pattern can be expressed make it a valuable decorating tool for any size or shape of room.

Left Good velvet has a rich and timeless quality that complements a traditional or modern design.

PRINCIPLES OF FABRICS

The colours and textures of fabrics can bring light, pattern and focus to a decorative scheme

DESIGNING WITH FABRIC

Fabric, perhaps more than any other material, offers an immense variety of ways to transform a room. It can redefine furniture, walls, windows and floors, provide links or demarcations between individual rooms or areas within them – and it can control the amount and quality of light in an interior.

Fabric is able to soften the hardness of architectural lines, yet accentuate individual forms. It is an important source of colour, pattern and texture, able to play a major role in influencing the style and mood of a room.

NATURAL FIBRES

The diversity of fabrics for interior design is almost alarmingly great. Traditional natural fabrics, such as cotton and silk, are complemented by a range of modern fibres, each of which possesses strong and weak points. The properties of individual fabrics – strength, elasticity, durability, resistance to stains and moisture – are considerations as important as their appearance, as they influence the long-term success of a design scheme.

Fabrics derived from natural fibres, such as cotton, linen, silk and wool, come from vegetable and animal sources and maintain their strong associations with the living world. Cotton is a very versatile material, available in a wide range of weights, textures and colours. It is generally tough, resilient and practical, and works well for most types of upholstery. Striped cotton prints are traditional in a conservatory, for example, where indoor and outdoor use, strong sunlight and variation in temperature can all take their toll on fabrics. Calicoes – lightweight, absorbent and washable – originated in India and were brought to England in the 17th century. They became very fashionable for clothing and furnishings, and are still used for curtains and cushions. Cotton can also produce delicate, fine fabrics, however, such as muslin, which will float in the breeze from a window and flow harmoniously around a particular shape.

Fabrics, unsurprisingly, have strong associations with the places where they were produced. Alsace, for example, is a major centre for the production of silk, linen, cotton and wool: the characteristic cotton Kelsch is usually woven in varying checks of red and white or blue and white. The simple pattern brings a crispness to curtains or bedlinen that suits informal surroundings.

A considered uniformity can be achieved by using one colour throughout a design scheme. The austerity of this white sitting room is alleviated by the use of informal loose cotton covers to soften the outlines of the three armchairs.

Linen, which is derived from flax, is less widely grown than cotton; it is a more complex fabric, and therefore more expensive to produce – even though it is often blended with other fibres, such as cotton, to reduce its cost and increase its suppleness. It is strong and hard wearing, ideal for throws and curtains, while Irish linen is renowned as the fabric used for some of the finest bedclothes and tablecloths. A delicate tracery of cotton insertion lace to edge a white linen pillow or cushion is a classic textural complement. It brings air and freshness to a heavy fabric.

Silk is the finest, smoothest and strongest of the natural fibres. It dyes well and drapes beautifully, making it ideal for a range of design applications, such as vibrant, colourful throws or hangings to offset the natural tones of wicker or wood. It shimmers and reflects light obliquely, making it a useful focal point for artificial coloured light, or in an interior with plenty of natural light. Pure silk must be kept away from direct sunlight, however, as it will fade and deteriorate. It is often mixed with wool or linen for durability and can bring an exotic hint of the East to a traditional sofa or bedroom.

Wool is a warm, comforting fabric, often blended with linen or silk for use in soft furnishings. Its warmth is created by protein structures of fibres and the 'crimp' that holds air between them. It is hard wearing – an excellent fabric for rugs or carpets – and now that recent manufacturing processes have reduced its tendency to shrink, so washing it has become easier. The natural associations of wool work particularly well with cool stone flags or ceramic tiles, where it introduces a welcome textural accent that is consistent with the theme.

MANMADE FIBRES

Natural fibres that have been regenerated and chemically treated are known as manmade fibres. Acetate and viscose rayon, for example, are made from treated plant cellulose, the threads of which are then twisted together to form a yarn. They are inexpensive to produce, easy to look after and provide a practical alternative to more expensive natural fabrics. Resistant to shrinkage and moth infestation, manmade fibres possess a soft, silky feel and drape well. Consequently, they are often used to imitate silk, resulting in fabrics such as brocade and moiré.

SYNTHETIC FABRICS

As their name suggests, synthetic fibres are derived from chemicals. Although they were first developed as cheap substitutes for natural fibres, the range of high-quality synthetics is now so impressive that their unique properties have started to turn some of them into a first choice for furnishings.

Acrylic has the bulk and feel of wool but is light and soft. Strong and crease-resistant, it is often mixed with wool or cotton – dralon velvet is a particularly well-known form. Nylon, the first synthetic fibre (its name referring to the fact that it was invented in New York and London at the same time), is made from chemical products of either coal or petroleum. Like acrylic, it is strong, light, easy to look after and can be woven into voile, lace, net, satin or seersucker. Another synthetic fibre, polyester, has long been used as an inexpensive imitation for wool, silk, cotton and linen. Hard wearing and crease-resistant, it is often mixed with cotton. Polyester net works particularly well as a window dressing, as it is not affected by strong sunlight. Although synthetic fibres lack the depth of totally natural ones, their modern derivatives are now worth serious consideration for use in at least part of an interior scheme.

FABRIC CONSTRUCTION

The characteristics of a fabric depend as much on the way it is constructed as they do on the fibres themselves. The four basic methods used to create fabric are weaving (the most common), twisting, knitting and felting. Each of these

methods produces a completely different type of texture in the finished fabric. The networks of weaves, intricacies of lace, textures of pile – and, of course, the colours chosen to implement them – create the patterns that are characteristic of each.

Weave is the interlacing of two sets of threads across one another at right angles. Lengthways threads, or warp, intersect the crosswise threads, or weft, in structures ranging from the simple to the intricate. Woven fabrics have integral textures, which can provide the illusion of pattern; this in turn may be enhanced by different weights of thread or flecks of colour.

Plain weaves, in which the weft threads go under and over the warp threads, produce fabrics such as muslin, calico, hessian and gingham. Taffeta is a plain weave made from silk or silk-like fibres such as rayon. A more complex weave is made from a mixture of fine and heavy yarns. These give the fabric a definite ribbed texture and a piece of furniture a clearly defined outline.

The staggered interlacing of two warp and weft threads creates twill, which can be much more flexible and easier to drape than a plain weave. This style of interlacing forms a diagonal pattern on each side of the cloth, and its distinctive interlocking 'V' is used in fabrics such as herringbone, denim, ticking and tartan.

Satin weaves, in contrast, minimize the over-and-under texture for a smooth, light-reflecting surface and a dull underside. A third set of yarns, pile weaves, create a three-dimensional fabric in a very similar way to a carpet. If the pile is a single continuous yarn that leaves loops on one-side of the fabric, the loops can be cut to create velvet, plush or chenille. Jacquard weaves, produced on a special loom, are particularly elaborate forms of weave.

Felt, the result of fibres being matted together into a web, has no grain or direction, so it can be cut, sewn or draped in any way without fear of fraying. Nets, macramé and laces are machine-knitted in a process which turns yarn into a serious of interlocking loops from a variety of 'stitches'.

FABRIC AND LIGHT

Pattern, texture and colour are not the only elements in a room that are influenced by fabrics. They affect the amount and quality of light in a space, both by modifying natural light at a window as curtains or blinds and by filtering artificial light as lampshades. In so doing, fabrics radically alter the way in which a room is perceived. There is, of course, also a structural dimension: window drapery can either highlight a window form or conceal it.

While the thickness and colour of a fabric used in a window treatment can determine the brightness of a room (pale, reflective fabrics, for example, will

Cushions can add the finishing touch to a room, harmonizing or contrasting with the colour of sofa and armchairs. Attractive borders and edges are often picked out in a complementary colour that occurs elsewhere in the design scheme.

KEYNOTES

- TEXTURAL WEAVES
- FINISHES
- REFLECTION
- ABSORPTION
- MOVEMENT
- ASSOCIATIONS
- DURABILITY

increase the brightness of a space by reflecting light rather than absorbing it), choosing them is a matter of individual preference. Be they fine voiles or dark, heavy velvets, a range of effects is possible, although a bedroom or bathroom may in any case require privacy.

ACCENTS AND DETAILS

The different fabrics available enable us to respond to the individual challenges of various spaces in a room. Fabric can be used on a large scale to add drama, create a feature wall or even to 'tent' a whole room. Small, decorative details can be particularly effective in subtly changing a mood, perhaps used as cushions or lampshades. It may be more appropriate to contrast colour or texture in carefully positioned accents. Lining cupboard doors with fabric in a kitchen, for example, brings a softer, rustic note

to a conventionally 'hard' area of the home. Solid wooden furniture complements supple fabrics such as muslin or cotton and provides a useful screen for all the domestic gubbins behind.

With so many experimental fabrics now available, particularly voiles that mix both natural and synthetic fibres with touches of ribbon, plastics, even artificial flowers, there is immense scope for imagination and creativity. Small lengths of such materials can be used to make up cushions and bolsters, or even sheer loose covers for summer. By making a considered colour choice you can easily create interesting accents in a room that will look soft and unforced. Embroidered and beaded fabrics can be used in the same way. Made up into cushions, they can introduce a textural contrast on a sofa with otherwise single colour cushions in a plain weave.

Embroidery has a luxuriant, fluid quality about it, and, because most of it is hand worked it has an antique flavour that sits happily in both traditional and contemporary interiors. From the lacy, open effect of drawn-thread work to the denser patterns of Scandinavian Hardanger or counted thread techniques, the use of such fabrics can highlight a theme or change our perception of a space.

The way a fabric is finished can determine its statement in a room. Plain cotton or linen curtains edged with a complementary textile – a wide velvet band, say – can make an impact that is completely different to that of the same curtains edged in silk. It will change the feel, even the sound, of the curtains as they close. Such textural contrasts, however minor, can be used to tie a scheme together in the most subtle way.

It is not always necessary to re-upholster an armchair that seems too dark for a new design scheme. A length of antique fabric, a paisley shawl or even a brightly coloured blanket folded over one arm will introduce a touch of glamour to transform the look.

PRINCIPLES OF PATTERN

*Pattern – woven-in texture or printed-on motif –
can change the emphasis or perspective in a room*

RIGHT **Under the influence of Napoleon, 'campaign furniture' became popular in the late 18th** century. Formal furniture shapes and chairs, often upholstered in a regimental striped fabric, are characteristic of the style.

PERCEIVING PATTERN

When we first look at a surface, we respond to its pattern. Whether this is inherent or specially applied, its legibility is determined by the contrast between one shape and another. Sometimes the effect is so subtle that we feel drawn to touch the surface to discover whether there is indeed a textural variation or whether the effect is purely visual. What we take to be pattern can often turn out to be an illusion: *trompe l'oeil*, for example, is in one sense pattern masquerading as texture.

We initially respond to a pattern in its most basic form – as lines, which may be vertical, horizontal or in random arrangement. The most expressive quality of a line is its direction, which will influence how we perceive the space; the stronger and straighter the line, the more powerful a feeling of movement it carries. The vertical columns of a Gothic cathedral, for example, form a repetitive pattern with a clearly defined upward momentum. Such a rhythm is challenging and dramatic, in contrast to horizontal lines, which rest and relax the observer. The ancient Chinese developed a system of rules and associations for patterns which were based on these

key differences. If horizontal lines are peaceful, diagonals are more vigorous and active, bringing a sense of movement and energy into a design.

Curves can evoke a variety of reactions: large, upward sweeps are inspiring in their effect and will draw us upwards in response; horizontal curves, closer to those of the sea, bring a sense of movement that is lulling and reflective rather than dramatic. In the same way that we need to create a linear balance in a room by considering the relationship of vertical and horizontal planes, so we should consider the movement in the lines of pattern in a scheme in order to achieve a sense of stability.

INTEGRAL PATTERN

Whether subtle or clearly defined, pattern is integral to the textures of fabrics. The process of weaving highlights pattern through the grouping of warp and weft threads in specific configurations; checks and stripes are the most basic and richly constructed, Jacquard fabrics the most complex. The latter create a textural pattern which is truly reversible, one side of the cloth being the 'positive' and the other the 'negative' of the design.

ABOVE **Toile de Jouy, developed in France at the end of the 18th century, is still popular today for its** romanticized pastoral scenes. The fabric is particularly favoured in bedrooms, where it can be used as wall covering, upholstery and curtains for the full dramatic effect.

Checks will introduce warmth and vitality to a small room. They may be incorporated in a fabric for duvet covers or curtains or featured in ceramic tiling in a shower room. A combination of rectangular and diagonal pattern (right) brings energy and movement to this clearly defined space.

Patterns can either be created during the weaving process or be stamped on afterwards. These are distinguished by the terms 'voided' and 'solid'. If a pattern is woven to leave areas of ground weave exposed, the fabric is referred to as voided. Exposing the ground weave in this way produces a 'self-coloured pattern' in the pile, so creating a damask effect. A traditional Indian fabric, damask was graced with beautifully descriptive names, reflecting the delicacy so prized in 18th-century Europe: 'Running Water', 'Evening Dew' and 'Textile Breezes' are a few examples. Brocade, a more elaborate form of damask, has figured patterns that are raised against the ground fabric by spooling additional coloured threads – often gold or silver – through the weave (which is an established embroidery technique). The two fabrics respond differently to the play of light: damask reflects light from its flat surface, while brocade, due to its raised pattern, casts a slight shadow.

Where bands of two different colours are incorporated into a weave, as in gingham, the chequerboard forms a half-tone. Several further colours can then be introduced to produce a much more complex design. As colour is diffused through the yarn, rather than applied directly to the surface, woven patterns can be deep and rich in texture and colour, providing excellent fabrics for heavy curtains and upholstery.

Single-coloured cloths that have not been embellished with woven or printed patterns are known collectively as plains. The visual impact of such fabrics derives from their colour and/or texture, and, as with velvets and herringbone, can be highly decorative.

Character can often be brought to a design through its imperfections; flecks of colour variation, for example, in organic fabrics or irregularities resulting when fabric is pressed or cut it in a decorative manner. Some plains, such as silks and velvets, may be dyed in one colour but reveal variations in tone as a result of 'hot pressing'. Moirés, for example, are ribbed fabrics given a clouded or watered effect as the result of the finished fabric being passed between heavy iron or copper rollers.

Patterns can also be applied to fabric by 'stitchery', a term covering the techniques of embroidery, appliqué, quilting and needlepoint. Often used for accents on a small scale, stitching introduces intricate designs that result in a more personalized effect.

PRINTED PATTERN

Most fabrics today are printed with some sort of design – abstract, floral or geometric. As a result, an enormous variety of printed cloths in different designs and colours is now available for interior schemes, including interpretations of many traditional designs, such as the famous toile de Jouy. These pictorial designs were extremely popular in France at the end of the 18th century, where some 300 manufacturers were involved in its production. Apart from *chinoiserie*, the most popular themes for the designs of these fabrics were romanticized depictions of rural life, political and social events such as the French Revolution and Napoleon in Egypt, and well-known theatrical scenes. A classic way of using toiles de Jouy involves decoration of all the surfaces of the room with the same fabric. Interestingly, this can confuse the eye into believing that the space is larger than it actually is, especially when mirrors and clever lighting are employed.

The earliest printing method for both fabrics and wallpapers involved the use of hand blocks and was at its peak in the West in the late 18th century. Although

The beauty of a faded English chintz will give any chair a successful facelift. Elegant without being obtrusive, this classic pattern sits comfortably within any decorative scheme.

The pale wood floor and washed walls of this sitting room provide a blank canvas for an assortment of chairs and sofas. Upholstered in a variety of patterned, colour-co-ordinated fabrics, the individual shapes of the chairs are cleverly displayed.

it was gradually superseded by roller printing over the next century, it was revived as a craft by William Morris and the Arts and Craft Movement. Still practised today, hand-block printing involves carving a design into a flat block of wood, dipping it in dye or ink and then painstakingly applying this directly to the cloth or paper – using only one colour per block. It is a labour-intensive and thus very expensive method, although some wallpapers and fabrics are still printed in this way – particularly those traditional designs for which the original blocks still exist.

Another hand process still in use today on textiles and papers is silk-screen printing. Like hand-block printing, only one colour can be added at a time, which involves making a screen that masks the areas not to be taken up by the ink. Ink or dye is pushed through the screen and left to dry, after which the next colour is added. Batik printing, in contrast, uses a 'resist' method, in which a pattern of wax or paste is applied to sections of the cloth to prevent dye being absorbed in those areas. After each dye bath, the wax is removed and the process repeated to form a design of more than one colour.

These processes allow for individuality, but are obviously unsuitable for mass-production techniques.

The vast majority of printed textiles are now produced using rotary screen printers, mechanized versions of hand silk-screen printing. Roller printing involves the engraving of a design on rollers, one for each colour. This method is chiefly used for long runs of inexpensive, mono- or two-colour cottons.

MOTIFS AND PATTERN

In motif fabrics, pattern is created in printed or woven designs through the systematic repetition of an image. This strong visual repetition makes them very attractive to use, because it is easy to co-ordinate a room by featuring the same motif on a variety of different elements. This can encompass architectural fixtures, creative displays of storage and pieces of furniture, although care should

Tranquility is an important factor in the design of any bedroom, and colours should be suitably muted and conducive to sleep. The popular combination of blue and white is adopted as the theme here – from the fabric headboard and matching cushions to the rug and small upholstered sofa in the window.

always be taken not to push the idea to extremes. Pattern works best if it is in proportion to the room in which it appears and is introduced gradually, gaining in presence through a cumulative impact. Motif fabric can draw inspiration from existing features, and adding carefully considered ornaments to enhance the motif can extend, strengthen and confirm a design.

There is a huge variety of motifs in use today – they combine innovation with historical interpretations and their strength lies in their ability to use classic designs without anachronism or conflict within a contemporary scheme. Many motifs carry hidden meanings or symbolism that often bring with them a complex mixture of associations. A wreath motif, for example, may represent sovereignty, honour, glory and victory; a palm tree, fame or victory; and a bee, industry and immortality. All of these motifs have been used in different periods of history – though, perhaps not surprisingly, particularly heavily during the French Empire. Plant motifs and floral images have been used extensively in fabric design over the centuries, ranging from naturalistic interpretations to more stylized floral displays. Traditional

damask motifs, for example, include arrangements of leaves, exotic fruits and ever-popular floral patterns.

Cotton chintz is a classic floral fabric that became extremely popular in both Britain and America during the 18th century. One of its most attractive characteristics is the mellowing and fading of its original bright colours from exposure to sunlight and laundering. This softening of the original scheme in fact helps to unify colour and pattern within the overall design, with the result that chintzes of the 18th and 19th century are in great demand. Manufacturers now artificially age fabrics to create the same effect by adjusting the dyes and chemical solutions; soaking fabric in weak tea is a simple – if irrevocable – way to achieve a similar result.

Originally, the majority of European overall patterned fabrics were decorated with stylized or naturalistic plant forms, such as grapevines, ivy, oak leaves and all sorts of flowers. Such different motifs work well together in establishing a natural theme, provided that the shapes are harmonious: sinuous and elegant or gently rounded. Think carefully about the size of individual motifs in relation to the area to be covered with fabric, paper or

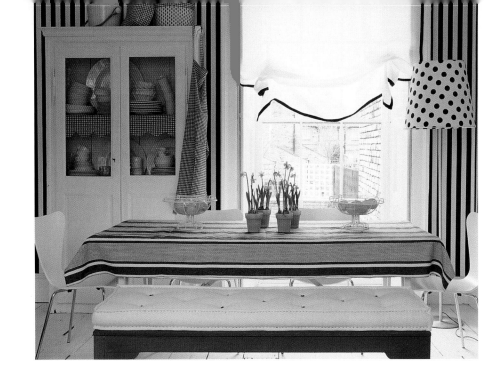

LEFT This Swedish-style bedroom is graced by two large windows, with a *lit-bateau* unusually placed at an angle between them. The pale blue-grey of its wooden frame echoes that of the mirror; the colour reappears in the stripe of bedlinen and cushion.

RIGHT The trick with pattern is to be daring. Mix spots with stripes and stripes with yet more stripes – even throw in a check or two – but keep the colour scheme the same.

BELOW Fabric with a large design is seen to best advantage against a single, co-ordinated block of colour. This grey wall balances the exuberant pattern of the curtains.

other material. A small design will translate more successfully to an accent – such as a cushion cover – or to a contained space – such as a small bedroom – but it may appear chaotic if used on a larger scale. Its constant repetition can also produce a mesmerizing, slightly vertiginous effect, which may distract from the overall theme.

Geometric designs vary from the simple to the complex, often drawing inspiration from classical references or Islamic mosaics. They work well on a wide range of surfaces, from ceramic tiles to fabrics, and include stripes (woven or printed) and checks (particularly tartans and ginghams). Ticking, a characteristically blue and white striped, woven linen or cotton, is a classic 'pure' geometric pattern which has remained in vogue and changed little since it first appeared in the late 18th century.

'Loosely' geometric-based patterns (as opposed to the 'pure' varieties described above) include trellis or latticework, the frames of which often carry a different style of motif – sinuous plants climbing through trellis, for example. The popularity of geometric designs is in part due to the recent influence of ethnic fabrics, such as the

dramatic 'kente' cloth of Ghana and Nigeria. The use of such textiles brings bold interpretations of colour into Western homes. Many traditional geometric designs are poised, elegant and ordered, and they can create an attractive symmetry and balance in interiors to calm the over-active mind. They influence our

awareness of size and shape, and may suggest that a room is taller and wider than it really is. Again, as with all pattern, scale must be borne in mind – geometric pattern used over large areas can easily disconcert or overwhelm, as it can if more than one geometric pattern is used in combination.

COMBINING TEXTURES AND STYLES

A wide range of fabrics gives us the freedom to develop imaginative combinations and styles

RIGHT **If an overall scheme is muted and uniform in colour, accessorizing with cushions in lively hues will** provide a new focus for the room. These cushions, with raised, self-coloured pattern, also introduce texture to the smoothness of the plain armchairs.

BALANCING THE LOOK

The sheer volume of fabrics and materials now available, and the ease with which we can access even more from different cultures and countries, allows us more flexibility to shape our own interior looks than ever before. The introduction of a number of different fabrics into a scheme enables us to establish a balance of old and new, East and West. The shape and style of furniture and accessories, and the colour tones of the space, can reinforce particular themes associated with the fabric. For example, the lacy, open structure of a wicker chair can echo a delicate floral cushion's rural theme by contributing to a general sense of lightness and air. Meanwhile, silk screens and neutral colours may evoke an exotic, oriental look, which can be reinforced by low level furnishings, clean lines and angular lamp bases, as illustrated in the room opposite. Old pieces of furniture may be covered with smart, crisp new fabrics that clearly define their authentic shapes, or a gently decaying, country house feel may be complemented by a soft pastel cotton or rich wool throw. Fabrics offer a useful way to bring different accents or whole themes into a design.

An intriguing method of balancing different themes is to reflect various interpretations of a particular motif throughout a space. Designs of the natural world, for example, range from elaborate combinations of birds, leaves and baskets of fruit (a feature of Jacobean needlework that became very popular in the late 18th and early 19th centuries), through to English chintz and the interlocking tendrils of Celtic knots and whorls. The celebrated paisley fabric, originally brought from India by Dutch traders and characterized by strong, deep colours, also draws inspiration from the natural world. Its typically rounded motifs are traditionally surrounded by background stems and spines. Paisley works particularly well as curtain fabric, where its own sense of movement is reflected in the physical effect. The natural theme of a design can be enhanced by being continued through a scheme into non-fabric interpretations: a gallery of botanical watercolours and sketches, for example, or Japanese prints of blossom and birds to introduce an Eastern note.

It is tempting to balance a traditional fabric with period furniture to create a scheme that is historically correct and

ABOVE **Playing with texture achieves unusual results. A couple of glazed chintz cushions provide a soft yet** solid contrast to the open framework of a simple rustic chair.

LEFT The old-fashioned femininity of this armchair in a loose cover of faded chintz is juxtaposed with a daringly bright orange stripe in the curtain at the window, an altogether more contemporary look.

LEFT The old-fashioned femininity of this armchair in a loose cover of faded chintz is juxtaposed with a daringly bright orange stripe in the curtain at the window, an altogether more contemporary look.

RIGHT Chintz, the name originally derived from the Indian word for such painted calicoes, now applies to a whole range of fabrics printed with designs of flowers and fruit. It has become synonymous with quintessential English design.

fits well with the architecture and structure of the space. Rather than trying to create a stage set, however, remember that most domestic space will need to encompass the paradoxes of modern life – including miscellaneous possessions that contrast with any tightly ordered scheme. Concern for complete historical accuracy may cause the loss of vitality from a space, and remove the stimulus of seeing how different fabrics, objects and textures interact.

DESIGNING WITH FABRICS

A particularly bold or flamboyant fabric design can be stunning in a domestic context, but it will only work if it balances other features of the room. It is important, therefore, to consider the degree to which the fabric will be the focal point, and whether other patterns and fabrics in the room will collaborate with the overall effect or simply confuse the mind and disturb the eye. The drama and vitality of African, native American and other ethnic fabrics can sometimes overwhelm a small space, so that the contribution of other ingredients in the design is distorted or lost. It is important to complement their bold colours and impact with some quieter, more serene

colours and simple lines of furniture and decoration. Wooden carvings or semi-sheer curtains made from Keralan cotton, woven with golden thread, for example, will enhance the ethnic mood. One advantage of an informal scheme such as this is that it never becomes too contained or precise – rather, it can evolve as time passes and possessions gradually accumulate.

The inspiration of traditional cultures in fabric design is nothing new: early in the 20th century, textile designers of the

Art Nouveau and Art Deco movements produced rich-coloured, geometric interpretations of Moroccan deep-wool Berber carpets, following exhibitions in Paris in 1917 and 1923. In Spain, too, the Moorish influence continues to be felt in elaborate wall hangings, tapestries and luxuriously patterned carpets. Kilims introduce an exotic note to a design and are also highly functional; their solid texture supplies comforting warmth to a cool stone or ceramic floor, or a protective, intimate note if used as

This charming bedroom is decorated with a delicate old-fashioned chintz, used on the walls and for the curtains and bedspread. Even the table is covered with a length of the fabric. Since the room is sparsely furnished, the overall effect is harmonious rather than fussy.

a wall hanging. Kilims can also be useful as a means of reducing sound from one room to the next.

A variety of different textures can be achieved not only between fabrics, but within them. A number of contemporary fabrics – particularly voiles – have started to incorporate intriguing materials with wonderfully exciting and individual results. Silks may be shot through with rope, or feathers and coconut husks woven into sheer panels. Although some can be used in upholstery, the most extreme fabrics are more limited in their use – often as room dividers or, if sheer enough, as blinds to diffuse light at the window. Many of these fabrics focus on texture and draw attention to how, through different weaving techniques, they have been fabricated. The contrast of one texture and fibre against another provides interest that can then be accentuated by using the play of light. Contrasting textural fabrics, such as raffia, ribbon and silk, juxtaposed in a cushion, say, will increase the effect of the whole. A more sophisticated note may be introduced by rubber, which is often mixed with other fabrics, as well as appearing as an innovative domestic material in its own right.

FABRICS AND DESIGN THEMES

While recognizing the diversity of the fabric styles and textures to which we have access, we should not forget that fabrics need to serve a useful as well as a decorative purpose in order to work well. For example, a British colonial style is often chosen for a porch or conservatory because it uses attractive materials, but on a more practical level, these materials are also suitable for their situation. The style's combination of different textures, such as wicker or rattan furniture and gently abrasive sea-grass matting are complemented by hardy canvas, striped cotton or crisp linen. The amount of natural light in a conservatory or porch suits such a natural and clean style, characterized by the smooth regularity of checks and stripes. Fabrics do fade if left in strong sunlight, so furnishings in exposed areas should not be your most treasured possessions, but attractive, homely items that regular use and the effects of light will enhance rather than spoil.

Fabrics' associations with previous decorative styles can prevent us from considering new ways of using them. Glazed chintz and velvets, for example, were both extremely popular in the late 19th century, so we connect the fabrics with a rather overbearing style of decoration. It is only recently that they have been developed as versatile interior fabrics suitable to modern interior schemes.

LEFT A mixture of upholstery fabrics and bold variety of cushions make the seating arrangement a focal point in this spacious living room. The scale of the patterning is in keeping with the proportions of the elegant space.

RIGHT A roller blind can be secured with something as simple as a length of rope. Its unexpected coarseness provides a pleasing contrast of texture against the smart geometric stripe.

items in their own right. The strong, harmonious blocks of colour in traditional Amish quilts have a compelling symmetry and bring a reassuring solidity to a room.

Certain classic fabrics have become icons of style that manage to avoid associations with any one place or time. A white damask tablecloth, for example, evokes a feeling of purity in a table setting and is not linked with a particular era. The integral pattern or motif may change, but the fabric will happily fit into most styles, allowing for individuality in place settings, table decorations

and napkins. A less formal or outdoor occasion might prefer Provençal table linen, a Mediterranean classic characterized by intricate pattern and bold colours from the local landscape.

The essential flexibility of fabrics – they can be installed and removed much more easily than lighting schemes or furniture, for example – makes them very useful in exploring a particular theme. As more styles are available now than ever before, we should not feel restricted to conventional combinations, but allow ourselves the freedom to experiment across the whole fabric range.

Contrast can be an important design inspiration, and both these materials can look dramatic if used in a contemporary room. New lighting techniques, too, have immensely improved our perception of their textures, whereas dimly-lit 19th-century homes relied upon the glaze of the chintz or the pile of the velvet to provide decorative highlights.

USING CLASSIC FABRICS

Quilts are a traditional way of blending several diverse fabrics and designs into a harmonious composition. The conventional patchwork relies on fabrics arranged purely by eye to achieve a pleasing result. Classic American quilting designs, with their gloriously evocative names such as 'Flying Geese' or 'Log Cabin', are worked according to the designated pattern. 'Flying Geese', for example, is a dynamic structure of small and large triangles that chase each other up the quilt. Either patterned or solid fabrics can be used for quilts, but generally the design reads best if a unifying colour is established and the patterns are variations on a theme. Quilts can be accommodated well in a room without stifling other elements, and indeed are often hung as decorative

DECORATING
WITH PATTERN

*Using different patterns together is a complex art,
but one that brings individuality to a room*

DEFINING THE SPACE

Pattern can radically influence how we view a particular space, whether it is used in fabrics or for another medium, such as mosaic or tiles. It is an extremely versatile ingredient of design, used to express continuity, or to highlight or conceal other features. It can appear accidental – for example on storage shelves where the items on display define their own rhythm – or highly contrived, to create a particular spatial illusion or effect. Consciously or not, we find a certain measure of repetition and order comforting, and we respond to pattern with interest and imagination.

When selecting a patterned fabric, it is important to consider various factors: the room's size, the quality of light it receives, the relationship of the new with any existing pattern. Be honest in assessing your aim – do you seek to highlight the room's best features or to distract attention from its weaker ones? Pattern has the potential to enhance a room, but it can do the opposite and spoil the effect if it is not chosen with care. This is why a fabric should never be selected in isolation; if it is to work, it must have visual coherence (which may mean contrast) with the rest of the design.

There are no hard and fast rules about using different patterns together. However, to succeed they need to be of distinctly different scales and to be linked by a co-ordinating colour that appears in both fabrics. For example, the Arts and Crafts theme of the bed hanging on the right complements the floral pattern on the walls. The large scale of the curtain does not seem to repeat, creating the impression of a picture appropriate to its narrative theme. The smaller pattern on the wallpaper repeats quickly, and this avoids conflict with the larger scene.

RHYTHM AND REPETITION

The underlying geometry of a wallpaper or fabric design plays a major role in our perception of a room. Vertical or horizontal lines, particularly if strongly repeated, will appear to increase a room's height or width; diagonal lines are more dynamic and active, evoking an impression of energy that seems to expand a surface. A repeated trellis pattern on a wall, for example, will give a greater sense of width and height, as it directs the eye upwards and outwards.

All such designs, however, depend for their success on the way in which they

Patterned wallpaper can be extremely subtle. The contrast of cool blue background and gold foliage pattern picks out the forms and colours of simple objects on the shelves. The warmth and movement in the leaf pattern counterpoints the clean lines and curved back of the brushed aluminium chair.

repeat. Some designs, such as the stripe used in the room on page 232, rely totally on repetiton for their effect. The geometry of a design is not always apparent when you first look at lengths of fabric and wallpaper on the roll – particularly the extent of its horizontal repeat. On the wall, most repeats give the sense of random pattern, but not all; some complex florals can actually read in a distinctly columnar fashion.

Rhythm and repetition is particularly noticeable on tiled floors and walls. Floor tiles made from natural materials such as terracottta, limestone or marble contain their own natural markings, but the primary impact of their pattern is geometric and, depending on how they are laid, can extend or contain the floor space. While the repetition of a single colour can produce a decorative but calm finish, colour highlights achieved by juxtaposing brick, slate or a soft red terracotta with paler limestone or sandstone can contribute to the rhythm of an overall design. However, the effect does not detract from the underlying geometry of the tiles themselves. For this reason, it is important to choose the correct size of tile; it needs to be in proportion with the available floor area,

**Masculine rooms are often deco-
rated in some form of check or
stripe. Their composure and order**
depends upon the successful inte-
gration of geometric patterns. The
regimented uniformity and subdued
colouring of this living room perhaps
reflect Napoleon's contribution to
interior design.

window panes, furniture and fittings,
and with the dimensions of the room.
The same is true of very small tiles, or
tesserae, which are a popular feature
around washbasins or kitchen sinks.
These can be delightful, but will look
fussy if used over too large an area and
with too small a repeating pattern.

The concept of displayed storage – a
pattern of objects consciously arranged
to bring a rhythm and focus to a room –
is not new – we have only to think of the
proud gallery of plates on a farmhouse
dresser or the elegant, leather-bound
volumes in a traditional library. Fashion
has now extended its scope to encompass relatively mundane articles, which
by their texture and shape can generate
an intriguing correspondence with one
another. Kitchens show ordinary 'tools
of the trade', implements displayed on
vertical racks; and smart conservatories
present an assortment of – often antique
– plant pots, watering cans, garden forks
and pruning knives arranged on carefully crafted benches. Glamorously
known as 'installations', the legacy of a
collecting hobby or family photographs
can also constitute this open look, in
which pattern is created less formally
than by a repeated motif.

LIGHT AND PATTERN

Because pattern directs eye, so it naturally creates focal points in a room,
although these may shift as light moves
during the day. As pools of coloured
light, generated by crystal prisms on a
sunny window ledge, take advantage of
this, adjusting their individual rainbows
as the hours pass, so reflective fabrics
and wall coverings can create a focus by
the way they reflect light in a room.
However, this device can easily be over-

done. If there are too many conflicting
surfaces, there may be tension between
the different light effects each produces.
Shiny fabrics reflect light and attract
attention, showing their colours more
clearly and strongly. Matt colours absorb
light and are more receding, but if they
are in rich, deep tones they will add
weight and depth to a scheme. A balanced combination of the two, either
within or between objects, is stimulating
yet not too draining on the eye.

LEFT **The vertical yellow and white stripes used in the decoration of this converted mews house** increase the sense of space and height. The width of the stripe is exactly that of a standard paint roller, and the evenness of stripe is achieved by dropping a plumb-line from the ceiling.

RIGHT **Stripes and checks often complement each other and seem to work well in functional rooms.** The effect of the horizontally striped blinds against the shelving units lightens the mood of this bathroom, and the sense of space is increased by the pale grey check pattern painted on the wooden floor.

SHAPING THE SPACE

Patterns can transform the relationship between different areas of a room by stressing connections through motif or background colour or, conversely, firmly differentiating them. Doing this too often may distort the desired effect; the space may either lose impact and appear dull or it may fragment into a number of incoherent, separate arenas. Perspective is also strongly influenced by pattern, especially a geometric one that either emphasizes or works against the structure of the building itself.

Striped fabric, for example, will allow the height or width of a piece of furniture, wall or room to be strengthened or exaggerated. The scale and strength of the stripe must be carefully judged against its colour contrast and in proportion to the size of the area involved. Too bold a stripe will be overwhelming and

have the effect of 'closing down' the space; too fine will run the risk of being insignificant. A check pattern – effectively stripes balanced against one another – has a similar but stronger effect, as the pattern is more robust and solid as a result of the addition of the opposing line. In the room on the previous page, a check fabric stretched on the walls gives a sturdiness and composure to the space that solid colour could not provide. Judiciously placed pictures reinforce the squares of the checks and give them balance.

Vertical stripes accentuate height and set a rhythm to the space. In the cleverly contrived scheme featured above, they also create a background that allows the awkwardly placed column to blend in. The large width of the stripe and the degree of contrast between its colours suits the size of the space.

Horizontal stripes accentuate width and introduce a clearly defined rhythm to a room: height is played down and the breadth of the room is emphasized. They can produce an illusion of solidity which momentarily fools the eye, as happens in the bathroom opposite. Here stripes are introduced in the form of roller blinds that pull down over the shelves, creating a false wall either side of the fireplace. The colours used in the striped blinds are taken from the geometric bathmat, while the floor is painted in a large-scale check, using a gentle earth colour and white, which in a muted way expands the appearance of the space. The lines and features of the room are vibrant and dynamic as a result of the bold use of a geometric design. If instead a flowing, floral pattern had been used as decoration, this would have been a softer, far less challenging space.

The bold rose-patterned wallpaper used for this small room could be overwhelming. However, it is given the freedom to work well on its own, with calming, off-white woodwork and a corresponding cushion cover.

CONTINUITY AND DIVISION

Recurring motifs, even in different patterns, can create strong relationships in a room. Floral wallpaper may appear too dominant to support complementary patterns, but there is no confrontation in the bedroom featured above. The scale of the mid-19th-century style of paper balances well with the window size and with the overall room. In so doing, the wallpaper avoids the risk of being reduced to the role of texture, which would happen if the pattern were too small and indistinct. The wallpaper is not allowed to get out of control, however, and relief is provided by the white woodwork and by the neutral underside of the cushion on the chair.

The stylized floral wallpaper on the right has an almost Jacobean quality, drawing on the sinuous branches, flowers and birds that characterize many such motifs. While both upholstery and wall patterns have a tonal and thematic link in themselves, the curved lines of the Chippendale style chair also enhance the sense of movement in the wall pattern. These lines in turn forge a further correspondence with the complementary fabric pattern on the seat.

While different patterns can become linked by the shape of a piece of furniture in this way, pattern can also distinguish a piece of furniture sharply from its background. It is important, therefore, that furniture treated in this way has a pleasing shape to define in the first place. The pattern of the fabric on the square, low-backed chair in the blue sitting room pictured overleaf, for example, relates to its background by using similar colours and stripes.

KEYNOTES

• VERTICALS AND HORIZONTALS

• PERSPECTIVE

• MOTIFS

• SHAPE AND FORM

• ADVANCING

• RECEDING

• MOVEMENT AND RHYTHM

This blue and white bedroom has been delineated by colour. The blue is used to highlight the beams and the wall behind the bed, while the remainder of the room – including furniture and window dressing – is kept white.

However, the sharp, vertical lines high-light the chair's shape, and the lighter pattern of the fabric draws it away from the recessive blue wall. The potential harshness of the stripe in such a context has been softened by the use of a flower motif, climbing like a honeysuckle between the stripes.

Although using different patterns together is not a simple art, it is not something to be shyed away from. Pattern introduces life and interest to a room, and if used well can set up exciting combinations of colour and form. It is nevertheless difficult to propose specific rules for decorating well with pattern, as so much depends on the constituents of the individual space. However, if proportion, other patterns, shape and light are all considered together, there is a useful base from which to proceed. The success of the pattern in context is essential to a good interior scheme.

Sometimes fabrics can be combined in a variety of colours and patterns by only a thin thread of unifying colour. In this corner, the blue background colour is echoed in the narrow stripe of the chair fabric and the darker shade of the curtain.

SOFT FURNISHING
INSPIRATIONS

*New fabrics and innovative ideas for their use have
revolutionized the concept of soft furnishings*

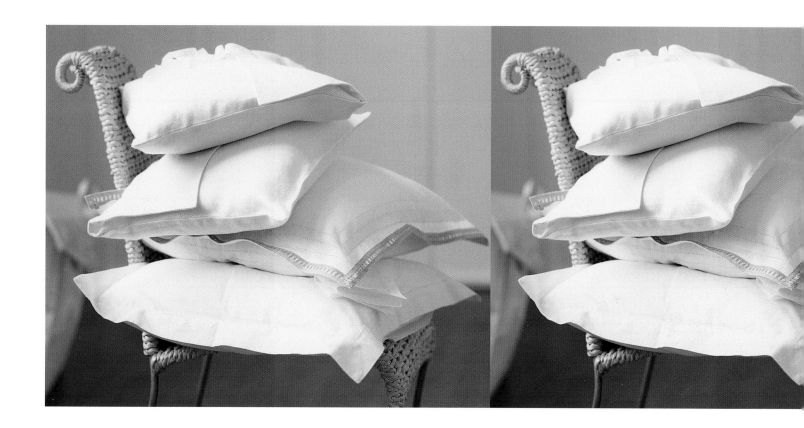

**Bed linen plays as important a role
in the design of the bedroom as the
covers and curtains. Pillowcases,**
duvet covers and sheets are now
available in every shape, size and
fabric. Their stripes, florals and patterns are designed to mix and match
with individual decorative schemes.
White linen remains the ultimate
luxury – either crisp and clean or
trimmed with embroidery or lace for
a softer, romantic effect.

CHOOSING A FABRIC

When choosing soft furnishings, there
needs to be some form of starting or
reference point. We can take inspiration
from the natural world or from the built
environment – for example, pebbles on
a beach, the shadows on an ancient wall
or the decorative features of a building.
The most conventional course of action
is to choose the main fabric for a room,
to be used for curtains or a sofa, and
then go on to select others that will work
with it, picking up a colour from the

original. It may be that the main fabric is
already in place and cannot be changed,
in which case its colours, pattern and
texture need careful consideration to
ensure a match for additional patterns.
A scheme can include many different
patterns of different scales and colours
and be very successful, but a link must
be made that pulls them all together.

This link is invariably colour. It does
not mean that you have to stick rigidly to
the same colour; provided that your
choice harmonizes, by being in the same

sector of the colour circle (see page 117), or is of a similar tone, it is unlikely to clash. Accent colour and contrast are also important to prevent a scheme from appearing bland. A contrasting design may be established, for example, when a strong colour is used on the walls and the furniture dressed with a white or pale fabric. This can create a crispness and a sense of definition within the space. It is likely, however, that there will be a pattern or detail somewhere – perhaps a

fabric, painting or other accessory – that will connect the two elements.

Fabrics are an extremely useful means of redressing any design imbalance in a room. If an overall colour scheme is too cool or too hard, it can be given warmth and softened by pattern while the integrity of the scheme is kept intact. In the room above, the walls are a strong, cool blue colour and the furnishings are predominantly white. These colours on their own might result in a cold, hard

ABOVE Antique bed linen and pillow-cases edged with lace, quilts of faded chintz, even a length of Victorian lace to drape over the bedhead can provide imaginative accents in a guest bedroom.

RIGHT A change of mood is created with a pile of colourful patterned cushions and low intimate lighting. Although ethnic fabrics are often difficult to use in an established design, isolating them in this way can be very successful.

LEFT **Fabric around a bed is often used to protect and cocoon, shielding from noise, light or** draughts of cold air. This high-sided cot is simply treated in co-ordinated linen and a quilt.

If a dominant fabric is shiny and highly reflective, light-absorbent velvets can be added to calm the effect. If a room is dark, it can be easily lightened with fabrics that are reflective. Some fabrics are only at their most beautiful when correct lighting is used. Dark, matt velvet almost sucks in light, whereas highly reflective satins and silks change colour in every crest and trough. You may decide to introduce voiles or sheer fabrics to make the most of available light, or to counteract the weight of heavier fabrics; and with flexible lighting sheers can be changed from being transparent to opaque.

Decisions about fabrics largely depend on how they will be used, the overall effect required, their cost and their practicality. The texture of a fabric says a great deal about how it can be used to best effect. Heavy fabrics that are stiff and showy and refuse to drape are obviously going to be more suited to upholstery than curtains. Smooth silks, though they may drape well, have a tissue paper crispness and saturated colour that is inappropriate for everyday use. Linen, on the other hand, is soft, hard wearing and folds well and can be used for upholstery and curtains. It has an

and contrasting scheme, yet everything in this room mitigates against such an effect. The colour contrast is strong, but soft patterns used in fabrics with romantic associations, such as the toile curtains and faded antique slip-cover, prevent the room from appearing severe. The soft frill to the pillow edge and the drape of the simple bed hanging add to the softness, while the gravity of the dark Victorian furniture and gilded frame

anchors the scheme. The gentle natural light that illuminates the room is softened through the sheer window treatment, and it highlights the hints of pink on the cushion and chair cover to warm up the cool blue.

LIGHT AND TEXTURE
The way light interacts with fabric can be designed purposefully into a scheme instead of just being a lucky coincidence.

extraordinary versatility and is one of today's most desirable furnishing fabrics.

Before the advent of central heating, the choice of soft furnishing fabrics took the seasons firmly into account. Heavy velvet curtains provided additional warmth in winter and insulation against leaking, badly fitting and draughty windows. They were traditionally replaced in summer by sheers, often swagged loosely over the same curtain pole, a

custom which effectively transformed the whole room.

Similar seasonal adaptations can be achieved with soft furnishing fabrics today, bringing a facelift to a room without the trouble and expense of redecoration. Rather like clothes in a wardrobe, the bright pastels of lightweight summer fabrics contrast with the thicker, more sober colours of winter. In a similar way, sofas and chairs that have

been upholstered in the darker, cosier colours of winter can be changed at a touch, replaced by a summer uniform of pastel cotton loose covers for the armchairs and a drape for the sofa. An element of warmth can be retained by placing a throw or a paisley shawl over one arm or the back of the sofa. The resulting change can be refreshing, satisfying and inexpensive.

The modern preference for a 'natural' look, epitomized by a focus on the multifarious shades of white, beige and taupe, have created new dimensions in fabric

design. In its role as the 'new colour', a fabric's feel and texture are now emphasized, rather than the focus being on the colour itself. Juxtaposing fabrics of different weight and surface texture is a device that is now widely used – for example, placing contrasting cushions on a sofa to introduce an intriguing and easily varied pattern. Upholstering seat and back cushions, perhaps with organic fabrics such as slub silk or linen, can also complement the pattern with a 'handwoven' texture, including natural flaws. The renewed popularity of drawn

Light and dark neutral tones in this room are brought to life by the clever mix of fabrics on the sofa. A white throw over its seat lightens the dark tones of wood elsewhere, and the patterned cushions pull together the whole colour palette.

RIGHT **Blinds are often used for difficult windows and work well with bold colours and pattern. The** wide stripe of the fabric used here imitates the width of the individual window panes, emphasizing their graphic effect.

threadwork and heavy, embroidered cloth – and the availability of a vast range of imaginative fabrics from which to choose – allows us to draw upon both antique and modern themes in shaping a textural design.

CURTAINS AND BLINDS

Curtains are obviously the most eye-catching use of fabric in a room. Their sheer extent concentrates a colour or pattern so that the whole design is inevitably influenced by them. The style and texture of the fabric chosen not only control the amount of light that filters into an interior, but also shape our overall impression of a room. An instant impression of quality is created by the thick lining and the heavy fall of a curtain, the width of its pelmet and length of its decorative fringe. Such window treatments are expensive and last a long time, evoking the sense of luxury and timelessness associated with grand living.

Blinds are a very contemporary window treatment, bringing a streamlined, compact look to a room. They are a very practical alternative to curtains, requiring less fabric and also taking up less space, making them particularly suitable

RIGHT **Texture, pattern, style and fibres of fabric are all so different that combining textiles is quite an** art. Silk taffeta with velvet, deep plush with tapestry, paisley with chintz – the key is to experiment until the combination works for you.

LEFT **Antique fabrics are part of our domestic heritage. They provide a sense of authority and tradition in** a scheme and are the perfect complements to old pieces of furniture. As restoration techniques become ever more successful, the opportunity for bringing such fabrics into regular use continues to grow.

Antique table and bed linen are popular collectibles, many pieces monogrammed or embroidered with family initials. Some pieces are so beautiful that they are properly reserved for special occasions, while others carry a sense of history into everyday use.

for a small room. They are simple to fix and can be cut to fit any awkward shape, so blinds are also an obvious choice for difficult windows, such as attic skylights. Blinds – roller, Roman, festoon or unusual modern designs – offer flexibility in light levels and can be successfully made from a range of fabrics. Sheers, for example, are particularly suitable for conservatories, where windows are numerous and there is a need to control the variable amount and quality of light through the day.

FLOOR FABRICS

Floor coverings are becoming more important and varied as the options available to us increase and we are no longer limited to wall-to-wall carpeting or bare boards. Designers are now increasingly experimenting with the materials that we put on the floor, and each idea opens up a new dimension to the overall look of a room. We can now choose the softness and mellow warmth of natural leather, the organic texture and sweet smell of seagrass, or the versatility of copra matting and its many popular derivatives. Alternatively, we can opt for a painted floor softened with mats and rag rugs, pastel cotton dhurries

from India or bright kilims coloured with vegetable dyes. Not just limited to floors, many of these textiles are equally adaptable as coverings for tables and chairs, as wall hangings or wherever there is a need for colour or texture.

ANTIQUE FABRICS

Antique fabrics add a different dimension elsewhere in a room. A scrap of faded chintz may even end up influencing an entire decorative scheme. Antique fabrics, like old furniture, lend to an interior a certain gravitas. There is a comfort in a well-worn, faded fabric, a sense of history and tradition, as well as, in many cases, an almost unique colour that can be difficult if not impossible to replicate today. Artificial ageing of fabrics, whether by washing them in a solution of weak tea or exposing them to strong sunlight, will help to emulate the faded elegance of antique chintz or linen. Whether used as accents or on a larger scale, antique fabrics can change the emphasis of a piece of furniture or a set of curtains in a room.

The art of passementerie – the decorative use of trimmings – dates back to the 17th century and is still used in Europe and North America in the

KEYNOTES

- FLEXIBILITY
- TEXTURAL CONTRAST
- PRACTICALITY
- ACCENTS
- TRIMMINGS AND BLINDS
- ENHANCING SHAPE
- ATMOSPHERE

The success of many a decorative effect lies in the detail – an imaginative border or trimming, a clever bow or simply a careful mix of colourways. This cushion tie provides a pretty and functional addition to the fabric design.

restoration of period houses. Braids and trimmings, such as tassels, fringing and piping, were originally used to cover the seams and edges of wall and bed hangings, while slip-covers protected furniture upholstered in fragile silks from dust and strong sunlight. The use of passementerie is no longer limited to traditional decoration. Its functional ornamentation now encompasses everything from ribbons and bows to bone, wood, feathers and seaside pebbles and shells. Textiles now have a broader definition, as a range of textural elements important to contemporary decoration.

USING FABRICS IN A DESIGN

As both the range and definition of fabrics is now so wide, their use is also an opportunity for enormous decorative entertainment. Artificial, coloured fur could lighten the severity of a traditional room, for example, or a chair upholstered in plastic could give an amusing edge to a modern scheme.

Trompe l'oeil, usually regarded as a paint effect, is another amusing and illusory trick that can be achieved with fabrics. A range of fake animal prints enable chairs and stools to be upholstered in a variety of 'skins', from leopard spots to zebra stripes and the more domesticated pony. Cottons printed with large architectural motifs, such as classical columns and capitals, can be used for curtains to make window space resemble a classical colonnade.

Similarly, the simple introduction of an ethnic fabric – a sari or ikat, for example – may change the focus of a design with its strong colours and bold patterns. It is not neccessary to limit the use of such fabrics to upholstery for ethnic furniture; they can also bring dynamism and vitality to a conventionally shaped piece. However, bright and dominant fabrics are best introduced locally and with some caution, so that they do not upset the balance of the room. Throws over tables and trunks, or to disguise unsightly chairs and concealed storage, often work better than large expanses of fabric in sofa covers or curtains.

The diversity of colours, patterns and textures of fabrics old and new make them a fascinating and varied decorating medium. Balanced with its space, light, colours and proportions, fabrics introduce an essential softness and visual delight to an interior.

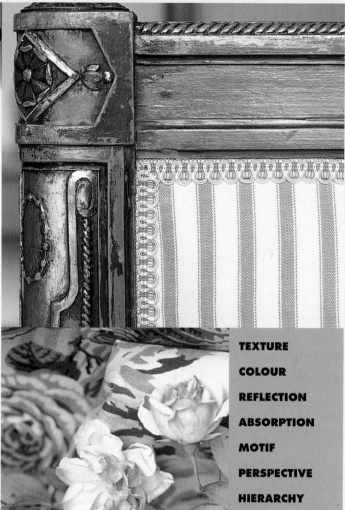

A SUMMARY OF **THE ESSENTIALS**

The timeless versatility of simple gingham check or herringbone weave carries an intrinsic longevity as well as beauty.

TEXTURE

COLOUR

REFLECTION

ABSORPTION

MOTIF

PERSPECTIVE

HIERARCHY

PROPORTION

RHYTHM

BALANCE

GLOSSARY
OF TERMS

Accent lighting A technique of lighting that highlights a special object or areas of interest.

Advancing colours Those colours closely relating to the warm hues of the spectrum which seem to come forward towards the viewer and so make a space seem smaller than it is.

Antiquing A decorative process that gives the surface of fabric or a material a false sense of age. It does this by imitating the discoloration caused by a build up of dust and grime over time.

Architrave A decorative moulding that surrounds a doorway, arch, window or wall panel.

Axis An imaginary straight line that passes through a ground plan, a building or an artwork. It provides a focus and a sense of movement in the space, and key features are arranged on either side of the axis to give an impression of balance. The places at which an axis begins and ends are known as datum points.

Backlight A form of lighting that is projected from behind and focused onto an object for dramatic visual effect. The object is left in silhouette with a highlight along its edge.

Bay A division of a building, either inside or out, which is created by supporting members, such as walls columns or buttresses. The demarcation of bays from the rest of the space through colour or texture may be a deliberate aim of a design.

Coffered ceiling A deep-panelled ceiling incorporating decorative panels. These are sunken into the ceiling fabric and usually presented in a geometric form.

Cornice A decorative moulding in plaster or wood that runs along the top of the wall to hide the join with the ceiling. It also describes a pelmet-like construction above a curtain arrangement.

Dado A design of beading or panelling fixed to the lower portion of the wall above the skirting.

Dado rail A decorative moulding that divides the upper and lower part of a wall. A common feature in period houses, it was originally designed to stop chairs from damaging the paint or plaster of the wall. It is also known as a chair rail.

Discharge lamps A type of lamp that produces light by passing an electric current through gases or metallic vapours contained in a bulb. The current produces a fluorescent discharge which iluminates the phosphor coating on the inside of the bulb or tube. The most commonly used type is mercury vapour. These lamps are very energy-efficient at high pressure.

Downlighter A fitting that throws light downwards into a room to provide a soft, indirect form of light. The lamps may be recessed, free-standing or surface mounted.

Eaves The lowest overhanging part of a pitched roof.

Façade The main elevation of a building; sometimes also one of its subsidiary elevations.

Filament A fine metal wire in a light bulb usually made of tungsten, which is heated to incandescence (the production of a glow) by the transmission of an electric current

Finial The terminal ormament of any projection. It most usually refers to the decorative end stop on a curtain pole.

Fluorescent tubes A form of lighting that uses the same mechanism as discharge lamps but that operates at lower pressures. The bulbs produce different coloured light from discharge lamps (usually slightly blue in tone). Traditionally regarded as utilitarian, they are now being used more widely in the home, especially where a flat wash-light is needed.

General or ambient lighting The type of illumination required for everyday use of a room. It may be provided by pendant lamps, uplighters, table or standard lamps.

Gilding A method of colouring the surface of materials gold, achieved through the application of gold leaf or gold paint. It can provide useful decorative highlights or increase reflective surfaces in a room to bring in more light.

GLS lamps or standard light bulbs These bulbs produce light with a red/yellow appearance. They enhance the tone of warm colours but dull cooler tones such as blues and greens. Although relatively cheap, the light quality is not as good as that of low-voltage tungsten.

Golden Section Also known as the Golden Ratio, the Golden Mean or the Divine Proportion, this is an ancient geometric concept that features in architecture, art and music. In mathematical terms, it is a means of dividing a certain length in such a way that the ratio of the longer part to the whole is the same as the ratio of the shorter part to the longer part.

Jib door A door made flush with the wall surface for aesthetic effect. It may be further concealed by being covered with patterned wallpaper or allowing the dado to run over it with no interruption.

Low voltage tungsten halogen lamp Types of lamp that produce a much more neutral or white light than the GLS lamp. They thus show colours more truthfully. These lamps are useful in a lighting scheme as they are energy-efficient, smaller and produce a precise light that is easier to direct.

Monochromatic Although literally meaning containing only one colour, in decorating terms monochromatic describes a scheme based around a single group or family of closely related colours. Many contemporary schemes use textural highlights to enhance monochromatic schemes based on neutral colours.

Mortar A mixture of sand, cement and/or lime and water used in structures for laying bricks, stones etc. It may be displayed to form a decorative accent in a scheme, and to establish a perspective in the space.

Motif A distinct or separable element in the design of a painting, sculpture or pattern.

Niche A recess in a wall, often used to hold a statue.

Receding colours Those colours closely relating to the cool hues of the spectrum which seem to move away from the viewer and so make a space appear to be larger than it is.

Riser The vertical piece connecting two treads of a stair.

Scalloping A specific, arching pattern of light and shadow on a wall, produced by lamps as part of a lighting scheme. The sharpness of the pattern depends on the fitting's distance away from the wall.

Task lighting A type of lighting for local or specific activities, usually employing direct light.

Wall-washing A technique of projecting light over the surface of a wall, bathing it with light. The light is then reflected off it into the room.

GENERAL
INDEX

ACKNOWLEDGEMENTS AND CREDITS

To Elinor Line, for her love, help and enormous patience; to Gabi Tubbs and the whole *Homes & Gardens* editorial team, whe helped create many of the images in the book; to Karen Howes whose picture knowledge was invaluable and to Simon Cavelle who shouldered much of the workload and without whose experience, both as a practitioner and teacher of interior design, this book would not have been written; to Nigel Soper for his elegant design; to Kathryn Cavelle and the KLC School of Design. And finally to Michael Dover for his foresight and enthusiasm and to Catherine Bradley who has worked so incredibly hard to shape this book.

2 Hotze Eisma/Taverne Agency/production Rianne Landstra; 8 IPC Magazines; 9 IPC Magazines; 11 Miriam Bleeker/Taverne Agency/production Frank Visser; 12 Galleria del Academia, Venice/AKG London; 14 The Art Archive; 15 Ben Johnson/Arcaid; 18 IPCMagazines; 20 IPC Magazines; 21 Fritz von der Schulenburg/Interior Archive, designer Mimmi O'Connell; 22 Fritz von der Schulenburg/Interior Archive, designer Mimmi O'Connell; 23 Simon Brown/Interior Archive; 24 IPC Magazines; 25 Jean Cazals/IPC Magazines, designer Claire Nelson/Nelson Seibold; 26 (top) IPC Magazines, (bottom) James Mortimer/Interior Archive; 27 IPC Magazines; 28 IPC Magazines; 30 Fritz von der Schulenburg/Interior Archive; 31 IPC Magazines; 32 Peter Dixon/IPC Magazines; 33 Fritz von der Schulenburg/Interior Archive, designer Charles Rennie Mackintosh; 34 Fritz von der Schulenburg/Interior Archive, architect Nico Rensch; 36 IPC Magazines; 37 James Merrell/IPC Magazines; 38 Andreas von Einsiedel/IPC Magazines, designer Kelly Hoppen; 39 Nicolas Bruant/IPC Magazines, designer Jacqueline Morabito; 40 James Merrell/IPC Magazines; 41 Jean Cazals/IPC Magazines, designer Claire Nelson; 42 Tim Beddow/Interior Archive, designer Dominique Keiffer; 43 Fritz von der Schulenburg/Interior Archive, designer Charles Rennie Mackintosh; 44 Andreas von Einsiedel/IPC Magazines, designer Kelly Hoppen; 45 Fritz von der Schulenburg/Interior Archive, designer Garouste & Bonetti; 46/47 Eduardo Munoz-Bayo/Interior Archive, architect Ron Arad; 47 Henry Wilson/Interior Archive, architect Mark Guard; 48 (top left) Fritz von der Schulenburg/Interior Archive, designer Emily Todhunter, (top right) Fritz von der Schulenburg/Interior Archive, designer Mimmi O'Connell, (bottom) Hannah Lewis/IPC Magazines; 49 Jan Baldwin/IPC Magazines; 50 Winfried Heinze/IPC Magazines; 51 Winfried Heinze/IPC Magazines, architect Caroline Langley; 52 Jean Cazals/IPC Magazines, designer Claire Nelson; 53 Henry Wilson/Interior Archive, architect Mark Guard; 54 (top) Jan Baldwin/IPC Magazines, designer Mark Brooks; (bottom) IPC Magazines; 55 IPC Magazines; 56 Peter Dixon/IPC Magazines; 57 Winfried Heinze/IPC Magazines; 58 Photographer Andreas von Einsiedel/IPC Magazines, designer Kelly Hoppen; 59 Tim Young/IPC Magazines; 60 Simon Upton/IPC Magazines, designer Jorge Villon; 62 Simon Brown/Interior Archive, Sir John Soane Museum; 63 IPC Magazines; 64 IPC Magazines; 65 Andreas von Einsiedel/IPC Magazines, designer Kelly Hoppen; 68 Scott Hawkins/IPC Magazines; 70 Photographer Jan Baldwin/IPC Magazines/Stephen Woodhams; 72 Henry Wilson/Interior Archive, architect Voon Yee Wong; 74 Gavin Cochrane/ lighting designs by Sally Storey (John Cullen Lighting); 75 IPC Magazines; 76 Caroline Arber/IPC Magazines; 77 Henry Wilson/Interior Archive, architect Voon Yee Wong; 78 James Morris/ lighting designs by Sally Storey (John Cullen Lighting); 79 Fritz von der Schulenburg/Interior Archive; 80 James Morris/lighting designs by Sally Storey (John Cullen Lighting); 81 James Morris/lighting designs by Sally Storey (John Cullen Lighting); 82 IPC Magazines; 83 IPC Magazines; 84/5 IPC Magazines; 86 Jan Baldwin/IPC Magazines; 87 John Mason/IPC Magazines; 88 Fritz von der Schulenburg/Interior Archive, designer de Padova; 89 (top) Jan Baldwin/IPC Magazines; (bottom)Jan Baldwin/IPC Magazines; 91 James Morris/ lighting designs by Sally Storey (John Cullen Lighting); 92 IPC Magazines; 93 Fritz von der Schulenburg/Interior Archive, designer Emily Todhunter; 94 Fritz von der Schulenburg/Interior Archive, designer de Padova; 95 Christopher Drake/IPC Magazines, designer Andrzej Zarzycki; 96 Jame Morris/lighting designs by Sally Storey (John Cullen Lighting); 97 Tim Young/IPC Magazines; 98 (top)Tim Young/IPC Magazines; (bottom) Jan Baldwin/IPC Magazines; 99 The Art Archive; 100 Fritz von der

Schulenburg/Interior Archive, architect Child & Co.; 102 (top) Wayne Vincent/Interior Archive/Jibby Beane; (bottom) Eduardo Munoz-Bayo/Interior Archive, architect Ron Arad; 103 IPC Magazines/Designer Nicholas Haslam; 104 IPC Magazines; 105 (top)James Merrell/IPC Magazines, (left) IPC Magazines, designer Nina Campbell;106 Andrew Wood/IPC Magazines; 107 IPC Magazines; 108 (top) Thomas Stewart/Interior Archive, designer Charlotte Packe; (bottom) Ken Hayden/Interior Archive/Dar Tamsna; 110 Photographer Pia Tryde/IPC Magazines, stylist Julia Bird; 112 Pia Tryde/IPC Magazines, designer Denise Hurst; 113 Pia Tryde/IPC Magazines, stylist Julia Bird; 114 IPC Magazines; (right) Fritz von der Schulenburg/Interior Archive, designer Richard Hudson; 115 IPC Magazines; 116 Pia Tryde/IPC Magazines; 117 Pia Tryde/IPC Magazines, designer Denise Hurst; 118 IPC Magazines; 119 (left) Henry Wilson/Interior Archive, architect Mark Guard; (top) Andrew Wood/IPC Magazines; (right) IPC Magazines; 120, 121Simon McBride/Interior Archive; 122 Pia Tryde/IPC Magazines; 123 Pia Tryde/IPC Magazines; 124 IPC Magazines; 125 IPC Magazines; 126 (right)Tom Leighton/IPC Magazines; (bottom) Pia Tryde/IPC Magazines; 127 IPC Magazines; 128 John Mason/IPC Magazines; 129 IPC Magazines; 130/1 Christopher Simon Sykes/Interior Archive, designer Maxine de la Falaise; 132 Fritz von der Schulenburg/Interior Archive; (right) John Mason/IPC Magazines; 133 IPC Magazines; 134 IPC Magazines; 135 Kim Sayer/IPC Magazines; 136 IPC Magazines; 137 Pia Tryde/IPC Magazines; 138 IPC Magazines; 139 (top) David George/IPC Magazines; (bottom) Pia Tryde/IPC Magazines, designer Denise Hurst;142 Pia Tryde/IPC Magazines; 143 (left) IPC Magazines; (bottom)John Mason/IPC Magazines; 144 IPC Magazines; (bottom right) Andrew Wood/IPC Magazines; 145 IPC Magazines; 146 David George/IPC Magazines; 147 The Art Archive; 148 Fritz von der Schulenburg/Interior Archive, designer Mongiardino; 149 (top) Simon Upton/Interior Archive, designer David Hare; (bottom)Fritz von der Schulenburg/Interior Archive, designer Mongiardino; 150 (top) John Mason/IPC Magazines; (bottom) Fritz von der Schulenburg/Interior Archive, designer Richard Hudson; 152 Alex Ramsay/IPC Magazines; 154 Andrew Wood/Interior Archive, designer Nicholas Haslam; 155 Fritz von der Schulenburg/Interior Archive, Claridge's; 156 (top) David Loftus/IPC Magazines; (bottom) Simon Upton/IPC Magazines; 157 Tim Young/IPC Magazines, designer Josephine Ryan; 158 Alex Ramsay/IPC Magazines; 159 Alex Ramsay/IPC Magazines; 160 IPC Magazines; 161 Alex Ramsay/IPC Magazines; 162 Henry Wilson/Interior Archive, architect Mark Guard; 163 Peter Dixon/IPC Magazines; 164 Fritz von der Schulenburg/Interior Archive; 165 (top left) IPC Magazines; (top right) Fritz von der Schulenburg/Interior Archive, designer Emily Todhunter; (bottom)Jan Baldwin/IPC Magazines; 166/7 Herbert Ypma/Interior Archive, architect Javier Sordo; 168 Richard Bryant/Arcaid, designer Frank Lloyd Wright; 169 The Art Archive;

170 Fritz von der Schulenburg/Interior Archive, architect Nico Rensch; 171 Hannah Lewis/IPC Magazines; 172 IPC Magazines; 173 IPC Magazines; 174 Hannah Lewis/IPC Magazines; 175 (top) IPC Magazines; (bottom) Alex Ramsay/IPC Magazines; 176 IPC Magazines; 177 Winfried Heinze/IPC Magazines, designer Bruno Triplet; 178 Pia Tryde/IPC Magazines; 179 Andreas von Einsiedel/IPC Magazines, designer Kelly Hoppen; 180 (left) Andreas von Einsiedel/IPC Magazines, designer Kelly Hoppen; 180 (right) Jan Baldwin/IPC Magazines; 181 James Mortimer/Interior Archive, architect Le Corbusier; 184 (left) Hannah Lewis/IPC Magazines; (right) IPC Magazines; 185 Andrew Wood/Interior Archive, designer Snap Dragon; 186 Fritz von der Schulenburg/Interior Archive, designer Le Corbusier; 187 Richard Einzig/Arcaid; 188 (top) Hannah Lewis/IPC Magazines; (bottom) Pia Tryde/IPC Magazines; (bottom) 189 IPC Magazines; 190 Pia Tryde/IPC Magazines; 191 Jeremy Young/IPC Magazines; 192 Pia Tryde/IPC Magazines; 193 IPC Magazines; 194 (left) IPC Magazines; (right)Jan Baldwin/IPC Magazines; 195 (top) Fritz von der Schulenburg/Interior Archive, designer Mimmi O'Connell; (bottom) IPC Magazines; 196 (top) Fritz von der Schulenburg/Interior Archive, Zuber; (bottom) Andrew Wood/Interior Archive, designer Nicholas Haslam; 198 IPC Magazines; 200 IPC Magazines; 201David George/IPC Magazines; 202 Pia Tryde/IPC Magazines; 204 IPC Magazines; 205 IPC Magazines; 206 IPC Magazines; 207 Fritz von der Schulenburg/Interior Archive, designer Mimmi O'Connell; 208 IPC Magazines; 209 IPC Magazines; 210/11 Alex Ramsay/IPC Magazines; 212 Jan Baldwin/IPC Magazines; 213 IPC Magazines; 214 Caroline Arber/IPC Magazines, designer Rachel Riley; 215 Pia Tryde/IPC Magazines; 217 IPC Magazines; 218 IPC Magazines; 219 Christopher Drake/IPC Magazines, stylist Katrin Cargill; (bottom) Simon Upton/IPC Magazines, designer Haywood Associates; 220 David Bennett & PSC/IPC Magazines, designer Cath Kidston; 221Polly Wreford/IPC Magazines, stylist Rebecca Duke; 222 IPC Magazines; 223 Pia Tryde/IPC Magazines; 224/5 Pia Tryde/Geoff and Gilly Newberry, fabrics by Bennison, London (daisy chain on oyster); 226 IPC Magazines; 227 IPC Magazines; 228 Jeremy Cockayne/Arcaid; 229 Fritz von der Schulenburg/Interior Archive, architect Quinlan Terry, designer Clifton Interiors; 230 Hotze Eisma/IPC Magazines; 231 IPC Magazines; 232 Fritz von der Schulenburg/Interior Archive, designer Richard Hudson; 233 IPC Magazines; 234 Pia Tryde/IPC Magazines; 235 Pia Tryde/Geoff and Gilly Newberry fabrics by Bennison (faded Malabar stripe on oyster); 236 IPC Magazines; 237 IPC Magazines; 238 Jan Baldwin/IPC Magazines; 239 Winfried Heinze/IPC Magazines; 240 Tim Evan-Cook/IPC Magazines; 241 IPC Magazines; 242 Peter Dixon/IPC Magazines; 243 IPC Magazines; 244 Alex Ramsay/IPC Magazines; 245 (top) Alex Ramsay/IPC Magazines; (bottom) Simon Whitmore/IPC Magazines, stylist Katrin Cargill; 246 IPC Magazines.